THE DEATH OF CHRIST

THE DEATH OF CHRIST

Fisher Humphreys

BROADMAN PRESS
Nashville Tennessee

For
Stephanie and Kenneth
agapetois teknois mou

Preface

I have written this book while possessed of two convictions. One I owe to Samuel J. Mikolaski: The Christian gospel will no longer be good news if the death of Jesus Christ ceases to be at its center. The other I owe to F. W. Dillistone: The theological meaning of Christ's death is so profound that it is worthy of a lifetime of imaginative and analytical exploration. I hope that reading this book will reinforce these convictions for readers as much as writing it has for me.

The fourth and fifth chapters are historical studies which throw light on the theory of atonement I am proposing. However, the theory can stand on its own, and readers who are not concerned about the history may wish to skip those chapters.

I want to record my gratitude to F. W. Dillistone for reading an early draft of this book and making comments on it, and for spending many hours discussing with me the meaning of Christ's sacrifice. I also wish to thank William Abraham, Claude L. Howe, Jr., Malcolm Tolbert, and Philip Wise for their very helpful suggestions. Five typists have worked on various drafts: Mrs. Dot Mohrlang, Miss Beth Firesheets, Mrs. Mary Golden, Mrs. Cynthia Wise, and Mrs. Diane Robbins. Because of them the book is much better than it otherwise would have been, though the responsibility for its shortcomings is mine.

Contents

Introduction

My purpose in writing this book can be stated very briefly. It is an attempt to explain the relationship between a single event in the ancient world and an often-repeated experience in the modern world. The event in the ancient world was the death of Jesus of Nazareth. The experience in the modern world is the experience of millions of Christian people who have been forgiven by God of their sins.

On the face of it, it seems improbable that there should be any relationship between these two. Yet it is the consistent testimony of Christian people that their experience was made possible by Christ's death. "He died that we might be forgiven, He died to make us good, That we might go at last to heaven, Saved by his precious blood." This testimony is a modern echo of the earliest known Christian tradition, which the apostle Paul recorded when he wrote: "I have passed on to you as of major importance the tradition I received, that Christ died for our sins" (1 Cor. 15:3, author's translation). We shall begin by looking at the ancient event.

The Event: Good Friday and Easter

It has always been difficult for Christians to realize that Jesus was a historical person, simply because they believe that in an important sense he transcended time. Certainly there was something timeless about him, and a man would hardly call himself a Christian if he did not think so. Nevertheless, it is very important for Christians to grasp the biblical truth that, whatever else Jesus may have been, he was a man who lived and died in a certain period of history. It is worth remembering that the first difficulty the church faced concerning Jesus was not a denial of his deity; it was a denial of his humanity. The writers of the New Testament adamantly opposed this heresy, insisting that anyone who says that Jesus Christ did not come *in the flesh* is not of God (see 1 John 4:1–3). It may seem odd to Christians today that the historicity, the flesh and blood, and the downright humanity of Jesus were so important to the early church. But the New Testament writers insisted vigorously that Jesus was a real man who lived in history.

Though the New Testament does not give a biography of Jesus, there is no doubt about one thing: he was executed by Roman soldiers. They crucified him near Jerusalem, in the spring of A.D. 33 or about that time. Crucifixion was a very painful form of death, and the Romans often employed it. Jesus was by no means the only person or the only Jew the Romans crucified.

When he died that spring day, there was every reason to suppose that the world had heard the last of him. Even though he had evidently been much appreciated as a teacher, he had written no books through which his ideas could be passed on. Although he had inspired a few Jews to be his followers, they were frightened by his arrest and deserted him before his execution. He left behind neither a mass popular movement nor a cadre of fanatical followers to carry on his work. He had, so far as is known, no contacts with political leaders through whom his moral influence might have continued for a time. In short, there was every reason for friends and enemies alike to believe that when

Jesus of Nazareth died, the world had heard the last of him.

As everyone knows, that is not the way things turned out. We Christians believe that three days after Jesus died, God raised him from the dead. Those who are not Christians do not accept this, but they too realize that the influence of Jesus, far from having been extinguished by his death, has continued to affect the lives of millions of people and in fact to shape Western culture and civilization until this day. The man who wrote no books has been the subject of tens of thousands of them. The man who left no organization or movement is worshiped today by the members of the largest and oldest existing institution in the Western world, the Christian church.

In view of all this, it is not surprising to find that many Christians lose sight of the historicity of Jesus. In this book we want to avoid that mistake. And so we begin with a straightforward statement: About the year 33, in the springtime, Jesus of Nazareth was crucified. Throughout the book we shall continue to inquire into the meaning of that event.

Here one other observation needs to be made. Throughout this book we are going to use phrases like "the sacrifice of Christ" and "the death of Jesus." By them we refer to this historical event. But in using them we do not intend to separate Jesus' death from other aspects of his life such as his teachings, his healings, or his resurrection. The passion, dying, death, burial, and resurrection of Jesus are in a real sense bound together as a single event, and that event in turn is one piece with his entire life. Our use of phrases like "Christ's crucifixion" is intended to convey the importance of the final days of his life on earth, not to minimize the importance of the rest of his life to which they are indissolubly linked.

The Experience: Being Forgiven

Now we turn our attention for a moment away from the ancient world and to the modern world. Hundreds of millions of people today confess that they are Christians. Naturally it is difficult to describe briefly what this means to all these people, but it would be pretty accurate to say that they believe God has forgiven them of their sins. Forgiveness is the normal if not quite the unanimous experience of all the people who think of themselves as followers of Jesus Christ.

I can best be more specific about the experience of forgiveness by speaking of my own experience. At a time in my life when I was not interested in God, I heard a sermon in which it was said that the deepest need of all men is to have a personal relationship to God. The sermon went on to say that this is impossible because men have rejected God by their sins; nevertheless, they could be forgiven of their sins because Jesus died for them and rose again. The preacher said that this forgiveness is available to those who will accept Jesus as their Savior.

I responded affirmatively to this message, as so many people before and since have responded to similar sermons, and found to my great surprise a confidence in God that I had previously not even anticipated as possible. Until today, more than twenty years later, that experience remains the most pivotal of my life. My life is what it is in large measure because of that experience and because of things which have grown out of it, including especially my participating in the life of the Christian church. My experience is not unusual; hundreds of millions of other Christians have had a similar experience.

The sermon I heard twenty years ago contained a number of assumptions which could be challenged. An atheist would of course challenge the existence of God. A humanist might doubt whether men are as sinful as all that, and a behaviorist might question whether men are in any case responsible for their behavior. A historian would question whether Jesus was really resurrected. I regard each of these questions as very important, and I feel that it is important for Christians to respond to them. However, that is not the purpose of this book. Here we shall assume that the experience occurs and that the Christian description of it as being forgiven by God is accurate.

There is nothing special about the word *forgiveness* in this description. What I experienced could be called becoming a Christian, being accepted by God, being reconciled to God, a new birth, or conversion. It is not the words or phrases but the experience they attempt to describe which concerns us here.

Nor are we concerned with emotions. Like any life-changing experience, this one is accompanied by certain feelings, but they are not of interest to us here. As a matter of fact, the feelings vary from one person to another in intensity and in content. For example, one Christian feels joy at being forgiven while another feels distress to find that his moral life was such that he was in need of forgiveness.

The experience of being forgiven, not a defense of it, terms for it, or emotions accompanying it, is our concern in this book.

The Explanation: The Relationship Between These Two

We have described an event from the history of the ancient world, the execution by imperial Rome of a man named Jesus in the city of Jerusalem in the spring of A.D. 33. We also have described an experience, shared by many millions of Christians since that time, of having been forgiven of their sins and accepted by God. The question we want to try to answer in this book is, How are these two related?

We shall begin by stating our question more specifically, since in this form it is ambiguous. As it stands it could call for two different kinds of answers. One kind of answer would state the relationship of Jesus' death to the Christian experience of forgiveness in psychological, sociological, or historical terms. For example, it is psychologically true that a profound sense of forgiveness comes to people who meditate upon the sacrifice of Christ and allow their lives to be shaped by the influence of his love. Or again, it is sociologically true that the death of Christ was a deed of such heroic proportions that it inspired a group of people to unite into a new society to remember what Christ had done. And it is historically true that through the centuries this society, the church, has continued to exist and to inspire in men a confidence in God and his goodness.

Our concern in this book is not for the psychological, sociological, or historical relationships between the cross and forgiveness; our concern is for the theological relationship. We are asking a bolder question: Before God, what is the relation of the death of Jesus to Christian forgiveness? Our intention is to find a theological explanation of Christ's death and resurrection.

In other words, our investigation is entirely a theological one. We are convinced that theological enquiry is an important enterprise for the Christian faith. For many Christians it is imperative. Nevertheless, there are more important matters, and we certainly believe that the work of God in Christ and the Christian experience of forgiveness have a priority over our theological reflection on them. The realities concerning which we think theologically are more important than our thinking about them.

We are not surprised to learn, therefore, that some Christians have never asked our question at all. They have been forgiven by God of their sins, but they feel no need for a theological explanation of Christ's death and resurrection. It is my judgment that if a Christian does not find the question forcing itself upon him, he is not obligated either to raise it in what would be for him an artificial manner or to attempt to answer it.

There are some Christians who go further and argue that our question is improper. Theories are all bad, they say, and divert men away from the primary issues of life. They feel that the link between Christ's history and the Christian's experience is too holy a mystery for man to examine. They argue that in matters of faith it is the heart and not the mind that is likely to find the truth. "The heart has its reasons which the reason cannot know," and the sooner one learns this the better; it is children who enter the kingdom of heaven first.

I am in sympathy with childlike innocence and with the reasons of the heart, but I do not think these objections to theological inquiry are valid. I reject them because I believe that the Christian message is to whole men, not just to their hearts or their minds. If this is true, then the search for theological explanation is a good thing. To inquire into the meaning of Christ's death is an activity which a thoughtful Christian finds natural simply because thinking is an ingredient of every important experience in his life. Furthermore, it meets a definite need in the lives of many Christians. If a thoughtful Christian cannot understand at all the connection between Christ's death and his own experience, he may begin to doubt if there is one. If this happens he will find that he is no longer able to affirm it, which means that his Christian faith will be substantially altered or possibly even lost.

It is for such persons that this book is written. They have been forgiven by God through the death of Christ, and they want and perhaps need to understand better what this means. I have been explicit about this because it seems to me that in our busy world it is best for an author to say plainly what he is trying to do and for whom to avoid wasting a reader's time. In our search for an answer we shall turn first to the inspired source of Christian knowledge, the New Testament.

1
Three New Testament Witnesses

In the New Testament the meaning of Christ's death is expressed in a variety of ways. In this chapter we shall examine three of the more fully developed of these. Each one occurs frequently in the New Testament; nevertheless, each one is associated with a particular writer or preacher. In the New Testament some of the explanations of Christ's death tend to fade into one another, but the three we shall examine are easily distinguished from one another because each appears in a very different setting from the others.

In examining these early explanations of Christ's death, we are interested in method as well as content. We shall observe how three men, Peter, Paul, and the writer of Hebrews, explain the meaning of Christ's death, and the technique each used to understand the atonement and to convey his understanding to others.

We shall also be attentive to the content of these biblical explanations, for we believe that they tell the truth about the meaning of Christ's death. Modern explanations of Christ's death are, I believe, attempts to understand and express the same truth which the New Testament writers understood and expressed long ago.

Peter: The Dawning of a New Age
in an Eschatological Setting

The New Testament is a book of great variety, yet Christians of all ages have assumed that there is a common thread running through it. However, it has been so difficult to specify what the common message is that some have despaired, pointing out that dealing with the peripheral elements might prove to be like peeling an onion; perhaps there is no core.

One celebrated attempt to discover the underlying New Testament message which has received wide acceptance was made by an English biblical scholar, C. H. Dodd. He compared the sermons summarized in Acts, which were the earliest Christian preaching, with isolated passages from the earliest Christian writing, namely, Paul's letters (1 Thessalonians, Galatians, 1 Corinthians, Romans). He discovered in these texts a common message which went like this: (1) The new age has dawned. (2) This has happened in the ministry, death, and resurrection of Jesus. (3) By virtue of the resurrection Jesus has been exalted at the right hand of God as the messianic head of the new Israel. (4) The Holy Spirit in the church is the sign of Christ's present power and glory. (5) The messianic age will shortly be consummated in the return of Christ. (6) Therefore, men must repent to receive forgiveness, the Holy Spirit, and the life of the new age.[1] This is the message which Peter, representing the church, preached, first at Pentecost and then later on numerous occasions, some of which are recorded in Acts.[2]

The first thing we notice about these sermons is that they are set in a context which is completely foreign to twentieth-century people. Their context is the eschatological hope of Jewish people in the first century that God would bring in a new age and a new world. Peter felt that this hope had been fulfilled in Jesus Christ. Two things had happened which made it clear to Peter that the old age was ending and the new beginning.

One was the coming of the Holy Spirit. In his first sermon Peter reminded his listeners that the prophet Joel had foretold that the coming of the Spirit would mark the end of the old age: "In the *last days* it shall be, God declares, that I will pour out my Spirit upon all flesh" (Acts 2:17). The arrival of the Spirit at Pentecost meant the new age was beginning.

The other event which showed that the new age had begun was the resurrection of Jesus from the dead. Peter stressed Jesus' resurrection in his sermon, although it cannot have made his message more palatable to his audience who were probably no more inclined to believe it than men are today. For Peter and his audience, it was axiomatic that the resurrection would mark the end of the age.

So Peter understood the life, death, and resurrection of Jesus in this particularly Jewish way: with Jesus the new age had dawned. The new age concept provided Peter with a link between the historical events of Jesus' life and the promise of divine forgiveness. How? Peter and his listeners all took it for granted that in the new age God would grant forgiveness to all men (Acts 2:39). Since Christ's resurrection and the arrival of the Holy Spirit show that the new age has begun, men can now be freely forgiven. For Peter and his audience, that was self-evident, because as Jews they shared a common concept of the new age.

But men today do not share these ideas. It is not their fault, but since they are not Jews living in the first century, these ideas, so far from being unquestioned assumptions as they were for Peter, are strange and foreign. Only by a deliberate imaginative leap can a modern man appreciate the eschatological way of understanding Jesus' life and death which was so natural for Jews of the first century. We today must provide a rationale for Peter's basic assumption, namely, that the new age has arrived.

This, then, is the earliest Christian explanation of the meaning of Jesus and of his death and resurrection: Jesus has inaugurated the new age of forgiveness. The response to Peter's preaching shows that this explanation of Jesus' death and resurrection was clear and convincing to Peter's listeners. Even so, it was not to be the last Christian explanation of Christ's death.

Paul: Justification in a Legal Setting

As a good Jew, Paul's greatest concern was to be righteous before God. He attempted to attain this position by zealously keeping the law of God recorded in the Old Testament. This was a legal maneuver to attain a legal standing. Paul obeyed the law so that God the lawgiver, who judges man's deeds by the law, would be compelled to judge Paul as righteous. A good judge would justify, or pronounce righteous, the man who obeyed the law, and conversely, a good judge would never justify a wicked man: "He who justifies the wicked and he who condemns the righteous are both alike an abomination to the Lord" (Prov. 17:15; see Ex. 23:7).

Contrary to what is sometimes said, Paul succeeded in keeping the law. He was more scrupulous and more zealous than his contemporaries (Gal. 1:13–14). He had every reason to feel confident that God would justify him.

Then he heard the Christian message that through Jesus God was forgiving sinners. Paul was sincerely offended. To him it must have seemed irresponsible to say that righteousness could come in any other way than by obeying the law. He was incensed at the suggestion that in God's sight the Jews with their law had no advantage over the Gentiles. He found the preaching about Jesus so outrageous that he determined to do his part in stopping it. If these Christians were going to oppose the holy law of God, Paul would oppose them.

But en route to Damascus to harass the Christians there, Paul encountered the living Christ and realized that what the Christians were preaching was true. He knew that his old way of life was doomed and that it could not provide him with righteousness. He ceased his attempts to achieve his own righteousness and humbly accepted a righteousness not his own, God's righteousness, provided to him as a free gift through the crucified and risen Christ.

For Paul, the connection between the historical event of Christ's sacrifice and his own experience of becoming a Christian, was that God had provided in Christ as a free gift the righteousness which Paul had tried to achieve on his own: "the righteousness of God is revealed" in the gospel, it is "manifested" there apart from the law, it is "shown" there and nowhere else (Rom. 1:17; 3:21; 3:25).

Paul, like Peter before him, validated his understanding of the meaning of Christ's death by quoting the Old Testament. In particular, he appealed to the example of Abraham who had been justified by his faith centuries before the law even existed. "The insight which he derives from Abraham's story, positively blasphemous even for non-Jewish ears, is that God justifies the ungodly" (Rom. 4:5).[3] In addition to validating his message by Scripture, Paul repeatedly defended it against the efforts of Judaizers to water it down or make it less radical.

But Paul never did give a rationale for his view which would satisfy people who do not share his presuppositions. He did not attempt to defend his conviction that Christ brought righteousness as a gift, for a simple reason. To him it was self-evident that if God chose to do such a thing as this, unexpected though it was, that was God's prerogative. After all, righteousness is God's, and if he chooses to share it with sinners as a free gift, who can say he shouldn't do it? "Astonishing as it may seem, in Romans 1:17 Paul speaks, *in one and the same sentence*, of the righteousness of God and that of the believer: nor are these two things, but one, God's righteousness." [4] "The distinctive feature of (Paul's) gospel is that God's righteousness is conveyed to believers." [5]

1. Yet it is precisely at this point that men today seriously question Paul's view. For one thing, is God really free to give righteousness to sinners? Must he not meet some conditions before he does this? This question, which comes up in many well-known Protestant theologies, never appears in Paul's letters: "Paul never raises the question discussed in later theology as to the conditions which God in his saving work had to satisfy so as to avoid damage to himself:" [6]

2. Again, modern men are troubled by the entire concept of righteousness as *given*. Surely, they say, it cannot be transferred from one person to another? Is it not fictitious to say that in Christ God imputes righteousness to sinful men? Is it not untrue or immoral or both for God to pronounce men "not guilty" when, in fact, they are guilty?

Yet these are precisely the things which Paul said; for as one distinguished scholar put it: "God attributes this righteousness to man who is a sinner and not righteous in himself." [7]

3. Part of the modern difficulty is due to the fact that, unlike modern men, Paul was thinking very much in legal terms, that is, in terms of the Jewish law. "God creates his righteousness for man, puts him in the right—man who apart from this verdict and act is lost, but now may have life in his sight. In all these turns of phrase God is and remains the judge, and man's relationship to him is conceived as a legal one." [8] It had been Paul's concern to secure a righteous

legal standing before God, and that is precisely what he found, except that it was God's righteousness, not his own, and it came by faith rather than by keeping the law. "The law remained a determining factor in his understanding of salvation even when he became a Christian and an apostle." [9]

The law was not the only factor in Paul's understanding of Christ; he understood salvation as peace with God, as reconciliation to God, as union with Christ, and in other ways. Nevertheless, the legal context was a major way Paul had of expressing the meaning of Christ and his cross: "But God shows his love for us in that while we were yet sinners Christ died for us. Since, therefore, we are now justified by his blood, much more shall we be saved by him from the wrath of God" (Rom. 5:8–9).

Hebrews: Sacrificial Cleansing
in a Ritual Setting

The four Gospels record that Jesus and his disciples traveled on more than one occasion to Jerusalem during pilgrimage time, and there is no record that Jesus ever discouraged his disciples from participating in Jewish rituals such as the daily sacrifices, the Passover, and the Day of Atonement. Following Jesus' ascension, the first Christians, who were of course all Jews, continued to participate in the fasts, prayers, and sacrifices of the Temple in Jerusalem. This practice probably continued for several years. As time went on, however, some Christians began to question whether it was proper for a follower of Jesus to participate in Jewish ritual practices. Eventually the view which said that Christians ought not to participate in Jewish rituals prevailed; Christians ceased participating, thereby becoming one of the very rare groups of people in the Roman world of the first century who offered no sacrifices at all.[10] A defense of this

somewhat eccentric behavior is found in the New Testament
in the book of Hebrews; one of its purposes was to convince
Jewish Christians that to return to practicing Jewish sacrifices would be a betrayal of their commitment to Christ.[11]

While the impetus for Christians to cease Jewish rituals
may have come from the influence of Gentiles in the early
church, it was not a lack of sympathy with Judaism that led
the author of Hebrews to reject the sacrifices of the Temple.
In fact, the author of Hebrews was himself a Jew and was
well informed about the sacrifices. He revered the Old Testament and honored the God of the Old Testament. Like the
Jewish priests themselves, he believed that forgiveness was
possible only when sacrificial blood had been shed (Heb.
9:22). Nevertheless, he rejected the Temple offerings in principle, and his principle was the entirely new one that Christ
by his cross had displaced the Jewish ritual sacrifices.[12]

Although Hebrews mentions several kinds of sacrifices, it
gives special attention to the Day of Atonement.[13] As described in Leviticus 16, the Day of Atonement was an annual
day of special sacrifices, its most distinctive characteristic
being that it was the only day in the year in which the
section of the Temple called the holy of holies was entered.
On the Day of Atonement the high priest first slaughtered a
bull and sprinkled some of its blood on the furniture of the
holy of holies as an offering to purify his own sins. Then he
slaughtered a goat and sprinkled some of its blood on the
same furniture to purify the sins of the people. Next he
mixed the blood of the two animals and put it on other
furniture as a further sin offering. He then confessed the sins
of the people over the head of a second goat called the
scapegoat (escape goat), which afterwards was released in
the desert to "bear all [Israel's] iniquities upon him to a
solitary land" (Lev. 16:22). Finally, the high priest

slaughtered various other animals and immolated their carcasses as sin offerings to God.

These rituals, so foreign and strange to modern man, were an important part of the religious life of the first Christians. The writer of Hebrews believed that when Jesus died he did what the high priest attempted to do on the Day of Atonement: he purified the people of their sin.

Except for the scapegoat, all the major aspects of the Day of Atonement are mentioned in Hebrews 9:1–14. The first five verses of the chapter describe the furniture in the holy of holies. Verses 6–10 describe how the high priest performed his duties on the Day of Atonement. Then we read:

> But when Christ appeared as a high priest of the good things that have come, then through the greater and more perfect tent (not made with hands, that is, not of this creation) he entered once for all into the Holy Place, taking not the blood of goats and calves but his own blood, thus securing an eternal redumption. For if the sprinkling of defiled persons with the blood of goats and bulls and with the ashes of a heifer sanctifies for the purification of the flesh, how much more shall the blood of Christ, who through the eternal Spirit offered himself without blemish to God, purify your conscience from dead works to serve the living God (vv. 11–14).

This passage explains why Christians do not need to participate in rituals like the Day of Atonement. Jesus offered a sacrifice so perfect that all other sacrifices have been rendered superfluous. Jesus' once-for-all sacrifice has purified the very consciences of men from all sins. Since they are now pure and will be presented to God without blemish, they have no further need to participate in the Day of Atonement. Therefore any Christian who feels that he needs the cleansing provided by the ritual of animal sacrifices is saying in effect that he does not really accept the true meaning of Jesus' death.

Peter felt a need for a new age; Paul felt a need for legal righteousness before God; the author of Hebrews felt a need for a sacrifice that, offered once and never repeated, would permanently cleanse men from all their sins. Like Peter and Paul before him, the author of Hebrews believed that his need was fully met in the death of Jesus. Here is how one writer expressed it:

Christ is understood as the true High Priest who entered heaven itself, the true Holy of Holies, and sprinkled his own blood there, performing a single effective act of purification. This purification was accomplished once for all, not repeated daily or annually, and it produced forgiveness not only for ritual infringements and unintentional sins, but cleansed even the consciences of sinful men. Therefore, it fulfilled the old Day of Atonement, and also surpassed and annulled it, being a far more effective means of dealing with sin. Everything was cleansed under the old Law by means of blood rituals, and the author argues that the blood of Christ is a far more efficacious agent for purification, or expiation.[14]

The presupposition upon which this understanding of the meaning of Christ's death rested was expressed by the author quite openly: "Without the shedding of blood there is no forgiveness of sins" (Heb. 9:22). It is difficult for modern people to understand this point of view, so difficult in fact that modern efforts to portray Christ's death as a sacrifice usually try to explain *how* a sacrifice cleanses from sins. But all such procedures are foreign to the writer of Hebrews, for the simple reason that all his life he had been so immersed in rituals like the Day of Atonement that he took it for granted that blood cleanses. Until we recognize that this was his presupposition, we cannot begin to see what he meant.

This brings us to one of the most important questions in our study. What value are these understandings of atonement to us if our presuppositions are not the same as those of the authors? We shall attempt to give an answer to that question in the following chapter.

NOTES

[1] C. H. Dodd, *The Apostolic Preaching and its Developments* (New York: Harper and Brothers, 1936), pp. 21–23.

[2] See Acts 2:14–41, 3:12–36, 4:10–12, 5:27–34, 10:34–43.

[3] Gunther Bornkamm, *Paul* (London: Hodder and Stoughton, 1971), p. 143.

[4] Bornkamm, p., 137.   [5] *Ibid.*, p. 136.

[6] *Ibid.*, p. 140.   [7] *Ibid.*, p. 137.

[8] *Ibid.*, p. 138.   [9] *Ibid.*, p. 115.

[10] Frances M. Young, *Sacrifice and the Death of Christ* (London: SPCK, 1975), p. 1.

[11] Young, p. 50.   [12] *Ibid.*, p. 50.

[13] "The all-important background (of Hebrews) is that of the day of Atonement when year by year a total expiation was made for the sins of the nation." F. W. Dillistone, *Traditional Symbols and the Contemporary World* (London: Epworth Press, 1973), p. 21.

[14] Young, p. 66.

2
Components of a Theory of Atonement

A theory of atonement is a theological explanation of the relationship between Jesus' death and the Christian experience of being forgiven. Every theory of atonement seeks to explain this relationship by comparing Jesus' death to some familiar factor in ordinary life. In other words, at the heart of a theory of atonement there is a familiar finite model employed to illuminate the infinite mystery of Christ's death. The model may be a real or imagined person, thing, event, or experience. The point is that at bottom a theory of atonement is saying, The death of Jesus is like some familiar reality. Thus in effect Peter said, The death and resurrection of Christ are like the dawning of a new age. Paul said, Christ's death and resurrection are like being legally justified in God's court. The author of Hebrews said, The death of Christ is like the sacrificial cleansing of the Day of Atonement.

There is a history behind every major model employed in a theory of atonement. Knowing the history can sometimes make a model more understandable. Also, each model appears first in a particular setting which, if understood, makes the model more effective. And each model carries with it certain assumptions which are usually implicit rather than explicit.

No single model can convey all the truth about the meaning of Christ's death. Therefore it is wise to be aware of the capabilities and limitations of any model we use.

In this chapter we shall give our attention to these six components of a theory of atonement: a model, its history, setting, presuppositions, capabilities, and limitations.

A Single Model

Whatever explanation one gives of the cross, one is in effect saying, "It is like this," or, "It is like that." When we compare the cross to an experience of the finite world, we are using that as a model of the cross. The usual procedure in providing an explanation of anything is to move from the known to the unknown, and that is what is done when a model is used for the atonement. It is a way of saying: The cross is a mystery, but we can understand some of it if we recognize that it is like this reality which is familiar to us.

Further, theological language is always language used in an extraordinary way. Because all language has as its basic reference the things and experiences of the world, to use language to speak of realities other than the world is to use it in an unusual way. Yet no other language is available to us. Earthly language is the only language we understand, so we have to use it. It is important to remember that talk about God is never directly descriptive; it is always a model.

We are interested in models for understanding the cross. But models may be used for purposes other than explanation. The only way we can discover what a model is for is to ask what the intention of the user is. Does he want to illustrate a point, to argue a case, to broaden the reader's appreciation of a truth he already understands, to persuade his reader to make a certain decision, to stir up the emotions of his reader, to make a personality come alive, or to raise a question? These are all legitimate uses for models, and there are others as well.

Our intention in this book is not to do any of these things, worthy though they are. Our purpose is simply to explain. We are looking for a model, not to illustrate or broaden appreciation or convince or urge decisions or persuade people about the cross, but simply to illuminate the meaning of the cross. Our goal is to throw as much light as possible on the great mystery of Jesus' sacrifice.

Three questions may be asked about explanatory models:

1. What happens if we refuse to use a model for the cross? The answer is that if we do this, we cannot say anything at all about what the cross means. We can still affirm that the cross is important, but unless we draw upon some model from our experience, we will be unable to explain its importance.

2. What happens if we attempt to state the theological meaning of Christ's death in direct descriptive language rather than with a model? The answer is that if we use a human word about a human experience (and that is all we have at our disposal), and if we say that this is *exactly* the meaning of an act of God, then we have either denied that God transcends what is human or else we have exalted a human experience to the transcendent level. That is, we are either atheists or idolaters! It was Paul Tillich who warned us so effectively of the danger of misusing symbols in an idolatrous way, treating as an ultimate concern something which is not ultimate at all.[1] To avoid this error we must admit frankly that whatever we say about God's act at the cross should be understood as being an indirect likeness to it, but not a direct description of it.

3. Why use a single model? Why not several? The answer is that it is in keeping with our purposes in this book to use a single model. It is our purpose to locate the familiar human experience which most closely resembles the sacrifice of

Christ. We intend to speak of Christ's death in the most basic and fundamental terms we can. For this purpose, a single model is very helpful.

Further, we are seeking a theological explanation of the cross which will have a maximum of clarity so that a thoughtful person can confidently affirm a connection between Christ's death and the Christian experience of forgiveness. A single model is especially helpful in an attempt to discover a clear meaning. If we used several models, we might jeopardize the clarity of our explanation; mixing metaphors often leads to muddled ideas.

Further, we hope to integrate various truths about the atonement into a unified theory. A single model will assist us as we try to weave the many strands into one explanation. If we are successful in this, in effect we will have illuminated other models with the light of our single model.

However, not all theological writing about the cross is intended to develop a unified explanation of this kind. For a theologian whose purposes are different, multiple models may be preferable to a single model. For example, the most learned and thought-provoking book published on this subject for many years employs no fewer than four pairs of models. I refer to *The Christian Understanding of Atonement* by F. W. Dillistone. It probes deeply into life to locate affinities between Christ's death and our human experience. By presenting so many suggestive affinities, Dillistone lifts our horizons and widens our vision. He helps us to develop a more sensitive appreciation for the great mystery of Christ's death. It would be difficult to overstate the help he has provided to students of the atonement.

In the present book as we employ a single model for the atonement, we must recognize that it cannot provide us with as wide an appreciation of the atonement as several models would. But we may hope that it will provide us with a basic, clea⌐, and unified theological explanation of the cross.

The History, Setting, and Presuppositions of a Model

1. Any major model for the atonement has a history. The model has moved from nonexistence to existence, perhaps to great importance, and possibly into obscurity again. Histories of the great models have been written, and of course models are continuing to develop in our own time.[2] Studying the history of a model can be very useful, particularly if it helps us to locate those elements in the life of a people or nation which gave rise to a particular model and thereby made it illuminating for understanding the meaning of the cross.

We might note, for example, that each of the three New Testament models we have examined was taken by early Christians from their Jewish background. "The symbols which had become so powerful to the Jews were taken over by the Christian as part of his heritage." [3] It was inevitable that the first Christians should do this, and it is likewise natural for Christians today to look to their common human experience for models to illuminate the cross.

In this book we are concerned about selecting a single model and using it to illuminate the meaning of the cross. This purpose can be achieved best if we compare and contrast our suggested model with others that have been used through the centuries. So in the next chapter, eight major theories of atonement will be described and criticized briefly. However, it will not be necessary to attempt a full history either of these eight models or of the doctrine of atonement generally in order to carry out our purpose.

On the other hand it will be helpful to have a brief history of the model which we intend to use since its history will provide us with a better understanding of it. That story will be told briefly in chapter 4.

Some theologians have doubted that the greatest models for God and his activity have any important history, feeling instead that they are universal and timeless. That view was propounded brilliantly by the late Austin Farrer in his Bampton Lectures entitled *The Glass of Vision*.[4] As attractive as Farrer's book is, it seems to me that no model for speaking about God is universally understood. This is true even of a classic model like God as shepherd. It is true that many people who never saw a sheep have developed an appreciation for the twenty-third Psalm. But if a man who never saw shepherds or sheep appreciates the psalm, he does so by making an imaginative leap. Perhaps he has been helped by paintings or by expositions of the psalm. Perhaps the psalm symbolizes some human need that is more or less universal, such as the need for a strong friend on whom we can depend fully, and this renders the psalm relevant to a modern man who has never seen a sheep. But a man who has never seen sheep cannot understand the psalm as its author did, because that image did not rise up naturally out of his life as it did out of the psalmist's life. The universality attributed to the model of God as a shepherd is therefore contrived, not natural. It depends upon the efforts of men who explain the meaning of the psalm in words and with pictures.

We hope to locate a model that rises up just as naturally out of our lives as that one did out of David's and which illuminates clearly the meaning of the cross of Jesus.

2. Each model we use to explain the meaning of Christ's death has been taken from a particular setting. A model may be used without regard to its setting, but its meaning is clearer when its setting is known. This is true of all three of

the New Testament models we examined. Peter's meaning is clearer if we are familiar with his eschatological hopes; Paul's understanding of justification is more illuminating if we are aware of his legal orientation. And we understand the sacrifice of Christ best if we recognize the ritual setting in which sacrifices first occurred.

The settings of these three New Testament models are fundamentally foreign to us. While there are some people today with an eschatological hope, very few (except Christians) expect God to establish a new age on earth. Virtually no one today participates in animal sacrifices. And while a legal setting is familiar to many people, particularly to lawyers, it is not Jewish law, with its concern for righteousness *before God* but a very different law, that they naturally identify with.

This means that we must make an imaginative leap in order to appreciate these three New Testament models. We must think ourselves back into the minds of first-century Jews, difficult as that may be, in order to sense what these models meant to their original users and recipients.

Try to imagine an entire nation tingling with expectancy that at any moment God will intervene, cure all illness, and establish political justice and liberty. Then imagine Peter seeing just how the resurrection and the coming of the Spirit fulfilled these national hopes.

Or imagine a disciplined, enthusiastic young man zealously pursuing a course of learning and scrupulously obeying the divine law which he sincerely believed would provide him with righteous standing before God. He overhears the story of the crucifixion of the prophet Jesus, which meant that Jesus was rejected by God. But then he learns that Jesus has been resurrected, a clear indication that Jesus has been accepted by God, and it dawns on him that a man can never become righteous by obedience to the law. His entire life is condemned, yet at the same time he sees with great clarity that in Jesus God has provided the only possible righteousness, his own, as a free gift to those who accept the condemnation of their self-righteousness and trust no longer in themselves but in God through Jesus.

Again, imagine a Jew for whom the Temple was the center of life and worship. His awareness of his impurities and sins has been trained by the law, and his only hope for forgiveness is to offer adequate and proper offerings, for he believes implicitly that forgiveness comes only by the shedding of blood. How good it is when he realizes that a new sacrifice has been offered which washes away once-for-all every sin for every man.

Historical imagination is indispensable if we are to appreciate the New Testament. Until we have seen the biblical models in their own settings, it is virtually useless to try to transfer them to settings with which we are familiar.

3. If it is important to know the history and setting of a model in order to appreciate it, it is even more important to know its presuppositions. Behind any model are certain assumptions, usually not expressed, which user and recipient must share if the model is to work.

For example, Peter assumed that what the world needed was the establishment of a new age. No half measures would help, no patching up of the old order. Apparently his hearers at Pentecost agreed, and perhaps some people today would agree that we need a new age. Many would not, for they are convinced that things are already working well enough. Apart from those whose Christian faith has trained them to think eschatologically, very few people today expect a new age to be established by God.

Paul presupposed that the most pressing issue in any

man's life is his need to be justified before God. But most
people today seem to feel that the opposite is true. They feel
that in view of the enormous amount of apparently pointless
innocent suffering, it is God and not man who needs to be
justified.

The writer of Hebrews is the only one of the three who has
stated his presupposition for us. As D. E. Nineham has written: "Similarly all New Testament talk about sacrifice would
have to be interpreted in the light of the doctrine felt by the
author of Hebrews as a fact too obvious to need justification:
that remission of sin is simply impossible without the shedding of some blood." [5] I do not know of anyone today who
naturally assumes, as the writer of Hebrews did, that sins can
be washed away only by the blood of sacrifices. Perhaps it is
not possible to presuppose this unless one offers animal
sacrifices as an ordinary part of his life.

Foreign as these presuppositions seem to us today, they
were probably shared by many people in the first-century
Jewish world, which is why the gospel found such a ready
audience among people on Pentecost and later. Even when
their claim was not accepted, their meaning was clear. What
they said was meaningful because their audience shared
their presupposition about eschatology, the law, and ritual.

The importance of shared presuppositions becomes evident if we realize that they include assumptions about limits
beyond which no argument need venture. One of the hardest
things for many people to accept, though it is clearly true
when we think about it, is that, theoretically and for human
beings, there is no final word about anything, no official
stopping place. We experience this with a child who continues to ask, "Why?", and who will not accept any word as
the last word. More sophisticated persons can do the same
thing. In our pluralistic world it often seems that some dis-

cussions never find a limit at which all the participants agree to halt.

But, in fact, we do not go on doubting everything or discussing endlessly. We come to some points where we are content to say, "I'll settle for that; I don't know any more basic way to put it; I can't take the exploration any further, and I don't want to; I have reached the limits at which I am satisfied to stop."

Part of the importance of the presuppositions behind the three New Testament models for the work of Christ lies in their containing limit concepts. In effect Peter was saying, "If you can't see the necessity for a new age, there's nothing more to be said." Paul was saying, "If you can't see the importance of being righteous before God, there's nothing more I can say." The writer of Hebrews was saying, "If you can't see that only blood washes away sin, there's nothing more to be said."

Therein lies our problem with these three models, for it is precisely these limit concepts, assumed by, built into, and indispensable for the models, that so many people today do not naturally accept. It is not that we today are perverse; I doubt if we are more perverse than first-century Jews. The problem lies elsewhere, in the simple fact that these three models arose, quite naturally and with all their presuppositions intact, out of a culture and life which their original users shared with their fellow Jews. They do not arise out of our culture and life, and we do not naturally share their presuppositions. Many modern men probably could not accept those presuppositions even if they tried. They tend to feel that sacrifices are repulsive and superstitious; they regard the desire for righteousness as quixotic if not neurotic perfectionism; they believe that constant anticipation of a new age is escapist.

It is not just skeptical people who find the presuppositions of these New Testament models difficult. Everyone does, including Christians, even very traditional ones. For example, conservative Christians have frequently tried to explain *how* a sacrifice can provide forgiveness. They have argued that the sacrifice should be understood in terms of propitiation (God's righteous wrath is appeased by the obedience of Christ) rather than of expiation (sacrifice cleanses a man from sin). I expect that the writer of Hebrews would have been puzzled by this argument; for he simply presupposed that sacrifice provides forgiveness, whereas this argument is trying to explain how this is true. In other words, for him this argument would have been superfluous, but it is very important to Christians today, whether conservative or not, precisely because they do not presuppose what he did. The same is true of Paul's view of justification and of Peter's conviction about a new age. The several theological debates that swirl around them provide conclusive evidence that many men today do not take for granted what first-century Christians presupposed.

This is certainly not to say that these models are untrue. That would be arrogant and wrongheaded. I believe that they are true, that they in fact express the most profound truths about the meaning of Jesus' death and resurrection. But they do so in terms of the culture and life of first-century Jews which we do not naturally share; they do not express their profound truth in terms of the culture and life common to twentieth-century men. This brings us back to the point we made when we discussed the setting of these models: What is needed today is a model for saying to modern men the same things that were said so effectively by these models to men in the first century. This means that we need a model whose setting is as natural to us as the eschatological, judicial, and ritual settings were to first-century Jews. We need to be as content to share the presuppositions of our model as first-century Jews were to share the presuppositions of these three biblical models.

The Capabilities and Limitations of a Model

A model clarifies the mystery of the cross by bringing to us some of its meaning in terms we already understand. No model can carry all the meaning of the cross. Therefore, in using a model, it is wise to fix carefully in our minds what it can and cannot convey, that is, its capabilities and limitations.

We have already said that the settings and presuppositions of the three New Testament models are distinctly Jewish and distinctly from the ancient world. Their first-century Jewish character was a major asset to them then, but it is a major limitation upon them now.

Now let us look at some of the more particular capabilities and limitations of these models. The new age concept is strong in its emphasis upon the newness of Christ's work. It is also vigorous in its presentation of the cosmic influence of it. And it shows a clear recognition of the importance of the resurrection of Jesus. It is limited, however, in explaining that though the new age has begun, still the old age continues. Further, the model does not contain even a hint that men need to respond to the new age ushered in by Jesus. This resulted at Pentecost in the curious situation of Peter's failing to urge a decision on his hearers, so that they had to ask him what response they should make (Acts 2:37–39).

Among the capabilities of the model of justification are its clear presentation that righteousness is a work of God and a free gift from God, and not in any sense a work of man. This is very clearly the case with Paul, who was converted, not so much from sin to righteousness, as from attempted self-righteousness to God's gift of righteousness. On the other hand, justification has its limitations. For example, it speaks of Christ's work for an individual rather than for an entire community so that the social implications of the cross may be neglected.

Sacrificial cleansing was the most fully developed model in the New Testament. It was capable of showing clearly the costliness of the work of Christ, and it also made clear that not just Christ's life but his death was important, as was that of the various sacrificial animals. On the other hand, since sacrifices were offered by man to God, the sacrificial model in itself does not communicate God's initiative in Christ. The writer of Hebrews had to take steps to counter the idea that men redeem themselves. Further, since all sacrifices were repeated with greater or lesser frequency, the writer of Hebrews had to spell out quite clearly the once-for-all nature of Jesus' sacrifice (Heb. 9:25–26).

Why is it so important to learn the capabilities and limitations of a model? The answer is that only in this way can we benefit fully from the light these models throw on the cross. If we were not aware of the limitations of these biblical models, we could easily draw false conclusions from them about Christ's death. For example, we could mistakenly conclude that no human response is needed since the new age is here, that Christ's work of justification has no social implications, and that what Jesus did was a work of man offering a sacrifice to God. We avoid these errors by bearing in mind that no model can say everything, and by being alert to the limitations of whatever model we use.

The Use of the Biblical Models

I have been arguing that the New Testament has passed on

to us several inspired models for the meaning of the cross, that these models arose naturally out of the life of first-century Judaism, and that we no longer naturally share in that life. If this is true, then there are four possible ways for us to deal with the New Testament models. We may repeat them, reject them, reinterpret them, or re-present them.

1. Repeating the New Testament models is the most conservative way of dealing with them, and it comes quite naturally to many people. They simply insist that certain models are found in the church's holy Scripture, which they are, then they unpack the teaching of the Bible about these models.

An excellent example of this is Leon Morris's treatment of the cross in Hebrews. Morris carefully documents from the book of Hebrews that Jesus' death was a unique sacrifice in several ways: it was once-for-all; it was offered in heaven not on earth; Christ's blood takes away grave moral sins while that of animals cannot; his sacrifice provides access to God while that of animals could not; his sacrifice was an act of obedience while that of animals was not.[6]

I share Morris's conviction that what we as Christians must do is to try to hear what God's Word is saying to us in the Bible. Nevertheless, I do not find this procedure satisfactory. The problem is that Morris never acknowledges that the sacrificial model is foreign to us, and so he makes no effort to bring to us the meaning it conveys. I read his words about Hebrews and wonder why these things are said, what all this means. How am I, a twentieth-century Christian, to know what it means to say that Jesus' sacrifice was offered in heaven? How can I appreciate the role of Christ's obedience in his sacrifice? Morris tells us what Hebrews says, but he does not tell us what it means. He sees that there is truth in Hebrews, but unfortunately he leaves it there, in Hebrews; he does not convey it to us here and now. That is the difficulty we face if we choose to repeat the New Testament models for the cross.

2. The second option for dealing with the New Testament models is to reject them. This option is chosen by those who feel that a model is actually false or at least that it is no longer true. Theodore R. Clark did this in his book, *Saved by His Life*. He seems to have found the model of sacrifice, especially bloody sacrifice, morally offensive and untrue, and he was concerned to eliminate it from Christian hymns and preaching. [7]

The problem with this procedure is that it will almost certainly involve losing the truth that these models convey. It concentrates on the limitations of the models and ignores their capabilities. It fails to understand that the models are true because it lacks the historical imagination to see the model as it appeared to its first-century Jewish users and recipients.

We cannot afford this option, for it will mean the loss of truth about the cross which we very much need. I certainly sympathize with Clark's moral hesitations, and I agree with him that the cross must be understood as a moral act, but I find his cure worse than the disease. Fortunately, we have other options available to us.

3. A third procedure is to interpret the New Testament models in ways that are meaningful to modern man. This is the option most often chosen by preachers and theologians alike. What is done in reinterpretation is to probe sensitively into modern life and find points of contact, at levels we may not ordinarily be aware of, with the biblical models for the cross. The old model is thus placed in a more familiar setting. In place of the presuppositions which modern men do not have, there is put either a rationale for the early presup-

positions or just new presuppositions altogether. In either case, the model is transferred into the modern world in workable condition.

I know of no more sensitive example of reinterpreting a New Testament model than a series of sermons preached in the 1870s by Henry Scott Holland.[8] Holland's concern was to explain the appropriateness of sacrifice. Religion, he said, is for good men in a good world to offer themselves to their good God, as good and joyous sacrifices. When man sinned, he robbed God of that gift. In the fallen world, the sacrifice that would have been joyous has become a gift of pain and tears. Man is so distorted by sin that he dreads to offer anything to God. And the sacrifices men do offer are unsatisfactory since no man is truly repentant. Could there be, asked Holland, a single man fully aware of sin's awfulness who would give himself to God? There was, and Christ sacrificed himself. His offering of praise to God is also our human offering because we are so closely united to him.

Holland made sacrifice attractive by removing it from the context of sin offerings and putting it in the context of gift offerings, a context of grateful worship rather than of propitiation or expiation. In so doing he made it understandable to modern men, and his view was a rich and profound one.

I have said that reinterpretation is the most popular option for dealing with the biblical models, and it is not hard to understand why. Its purpose is to take the ancient model and transform it so that it will speak to modern man. I feel, however, that its results are often unsatisfactory. Unless a person is predisposed to look with favor upon a biblical model, he is likely to feel doubly unhappy with a revised edition of one. The result of this procedure is often the precise opposite of what is needed. It may give us a modern message in an ancient model, when what is needed is the ancient message in a modern model. This is in some ways the case with Holland's sermons, good as they are. They say almost nothing about sin sacrifices. Now it is true that in ancient religions there were other kinds of sacrifices such as communion sacrifices and gift sacrifices, and Holland was in that sense justified in speaking of sacrifice as he did. But the purpose of sacrifice in the New Testament generally and in Hebrews particularly was to expiate sins so that man might be restored to God. On that important point Holland throws no light at all. His message is a modern one, though his model of sacrifice is taken from the ancient world of the Bible.

4. The fourth option we have concerning the New Testament models is to re-present their truth by using a modern model. We do this by being sensitive enough to the culture and life in which we ourselves share to recognize occurrences or experiences which are like Christ's death, and by using these to do for modern men what the New Testament models did for men of the ancient world. They are not just illustrations but actual parallels to Christ's work that throw light on the meaning of his work. Because they arise out of some familiar aspect of modern life, they obtain naturally, and no rationale is needed for their use. Because the presuppositions that accompany them are shared by modern men, they satisfy us, taking the discussion to limits at which we are content to stop.

It may be felt that our modern world is too superficial or too sinful to produce suitable models for theology. This objection is not as compelling as it first appears to be. After all, the life of Jews in the first century was not a perfect life, yet it produced a great many models for Christ's work which the church found satisfying, three of which we have examined.

What we do admit is that the modern world is so pluralistic that it is unlikely that everyone will share the presuppositions of any one model. That is one of the reasons that Dillistone and others continue to employ multiple models. Nevertheless, what we can do is select a model whose limit concepts we share with a number of people and use it to throw light for ourselves upon the death of Christ, hoping that others who do not share our presuppositions will seek out a model that can do the same for them.

A second objection to re-presenting the New Testament models with modern ones is that we are not authorized to replace the biblical models. But that is to misunderstand our procedure. We are not attempting to substitute new models for the old ones, but rather to let the truth of the old models speak to modern men by employing a model that has arisen out of our experience just as the New Testament models arose out of experiences of the first century. We are not getting rid of the older models. We want their message to become clear and convincing to us today. However, we want our acceptance of them to rest upon more than their antiquity, authority, and power in the past; we want it to rest upon their power to illuminate the cross for us today. I believe that they can do that if we use a modern model to see the meaning of the cross and then go on to see the biblical models in light of this modern one.

In any event, the real test for a methodology is not how convincingly it is described, but what it produces when it is put to use. So the value of the discussion here will be verified or falsified by the model from modern life which it is the purpose of this book to commend as valuable in helping us today to understand the meaning of Jesus' cross. First, however, we will survey some models of the cross used in the past and then look at the history of the model we believe to be so helpful.

NOTES

[1] Paul Tillich, *Systematic Theology* (Chicago: The University of Chicago Press, 1951), I, pp. 261–279.

[2] There are many good histories of the doctrine of atonement. A large one that has received deserved acclaim is *The Work of Christ* by R. S. Franks (London: Thomas Nelson and Sons, 1962). Two smaller ones are *The Doctrine of the Atonement* by J. K. Mosley (London: Duckworth, 1915), and *The Doctrine of the Work of Christ* by Sydney Cave (Nashville: Cokesbury Press, 1937). Even shorter histories appear in books like *No Cross, No Crown* by William Wolf (New York: Doubleday, 1957), and *Interpreting the Atonement* by Robert H. Culpepper (Grand Rapids: Eerdmans, 1966).

[3] Thomas Fawcett, *The Symbolic Language of Religion* (Minneapolis: Augsburg Publishing House, 1971), p. 219.

[4] Austin Farrer, *The Glass of Vision* (London: Dacre Press, 1948), Chapter Three on biblical images and Chapter Six on archetypes.

[5] D. E. Nineham, *New Testament Interpretation in an Historical Age* (London: Athlone Press, 1976), p. 19.

[6] Leon Morris, *The Cross in the New Testament* (Grand Rapids: Eerdmans, 1965), especially pp. 290–293.

[7] Theodore R. Clark, *Saved by His Life* (New York: Macmillan, 1959).

[8] Henry Scott Holland, *Four Sermons on the Sacrifice of the Cross* (London: Rivington's, 1879).

3
Theologians at Work

We are seeking a theological explanation of the meaning of Christ's death that will make clear how his death is related to the Christian experience of forgiveness. A theological explanation of Christ's death is technically known as a theory of atonement. Such a theory consists of a model taken from the ordinary world and used to explain the meaning of the extraordinary sacrifice of Christ. Every model has been taken from some particular setting. When that setting is not familiar to us, we must use historical imagination to grasp its meaning. The fact that a model appears in a setting that is foreign to ordinary modern life certainly does not mean that it is false, but it does mean that its explanatory power is less for modern man than it was for those who were familiar with its setting and shared its presuppositions.

We believe that the models of the New Testament tell us the truth about Jesus' death. How are we to employ them? If we merely repeat them, we are likely to leave their meaning unclear to all except biblical devotees who happen to have excellent historical imagination. If we reject them, we reveal our own lack of historical imagination and we forfeit their message. If we reinterpret them, we are very likely to end up with the worst result of all, a modern message in an ancient package. We have chosen, therefore, to re-present them, which means to look for a model which arises naturally out

of our ordinary life and which is capable of doing for us what
the New Testament models did for first-century Christians,
which is to provide a theological explanation for the meaning of Christ's death and resurrection.

In this chapter we are going to examine eight theologians
who wrote about Christ's death over a period of sixteen
centuries to locate their basic model. Most of them used
more than one model. In each case I have chosen a single
model in order to carry out our purpose of looking for a
single fundamental one for ourselves. We want especially to
notice the setting and presuppositions of their models,
though not necessarily their history. I intend to appraise
some of the capabilities and limitations of each one, which
will involve dealing with certain issues concerning Christ's
work for the first time. Our main purpose is to see if any of
these models will serve for us today. A secondary purpose is
to continue our observation of how theories of atonement
work.

Athanasius: The Deification of Human Nature

Athanasius was a bishop of Alexandria in the fourth century. While he was still young he wrote a book entitled *The
Incarnation*[1] in which he argued that Jesus was truly divine,
the incarnation of the eternal Word of God. Throughout his
long life Athanasius defended that view against Arius and
his successors who denied it. Humanly speaking it is due
largely to Athanasius that the church accepted the doctrine
that Christ was divine and Christianity was not reduced to
an exotic sect of Judaism.

Athanasius' theology was evangelical in that his concern
was chiefly for salvation. Nevertheless Athanasius lived and
worked in Alexandria, which was the intellectual center of
Neoplatonism, and inevitably he used terms and ways of

thinking which had originated in that philosophy. He did not thereby pervert the gospel. Rather he found in Neoplatonism a way to understand and express the gospel in terms that made it clear to his contemporaries.

Neoplatonism taught that every individual object is what it is because it participates in a transcendent reality. For example, a picture is beautiful because it participates in a transcendent reality which could be called *Beauty*. The nature of these transcendent realities was a matter of great interest to this philosophy.

Using Neoplatonic language, Athanasius taught that a man is a human being because he participates in *human nature*. He believed that the transcendent reality called *human nature* has been corrupted by the fall of Adam, and since it was corrupt it was on the way to death. Every human being is corrupt and destined for death since one could not be a human being unless he shared in human nature, which is corrupt and dying.

God loved men, said Athanasius, and he did not want to see them all perish; so he sent his Son to rescue them. He achieved this by uniting corrupt dying human nature to himself and thereby allowing it to share the incorruption and life of the *divine nature*. The union of the divine nature with human nature also meant that Christ was subject to death himself, but even his death played a role in the transformation of human nature and was inevitably overcome by the incorruption of the divine nature in the form of the resurrection. Athanasius expressed his view of Christ tersely this way: "He became man that we might become divine." [2]

Athanasius told various stories to illustrate his point. For example:

When a great king has entered into some great city and dwelt in one of the houses in it, such a city is then greatly honored, and no longer does any enemy or bandit come against it, but it is rather treated with regard because of the king who has taken up residence in one of its houses; so also is the case with the king of all. For since he has come to our realm and has dwelt in a body similar to ours, now every machination of the enemy against men has ceased and the corruption of death, which formerly had power over them, has been destroyed." [3]

This view emphasizes that the incarnation itself contributes to men's salvation, but Athanasius believed that Jesus' death also contributed to salvation because it was a reversal of death in men.

It would be difficult to exaggerate the achievement of Athanasius. He recognized the hopeless situation of man, and he stressed that God had done for man what man could not do on his own. He pictured salvation in terms that are morally appropriate; he showed that Christ's death, in spite of appearances, was a tremendous victory. He stressed that the kind of change that is needed in man is a fundamental change, one that reaches down into his basic nature. He held together the person and work of Christ, which many theologies have failed to do, by saying that both the incarnation and the death of Christ contribute to man's salvation. And he did all of this using the model of nature drawn from Neoplatonism which was familiar to his contemporaries.

But for us today, it is precisely this that precludes our explaining Christ's work in Athanasius' way, for we are not Neoplatonists. I do not know a single person who thinks naturally in terms of transcendent natures in which the individual objects of earth participate. If we want to affirm the things that Athanasius taught, we can do so only by employing a different model than his, one that arises out of contemporary life as his arose out of life in Alexandria in the fourth century.

Anselm: Christ's Vicarious Death

At the end of the eleventh century, Anselm, archbishop of Canterbury, wrote a book entitled *Why God Became Man* in which he rejected as morally inappropriate the popular theory that Jesus' death was a ransom paid to the devil. He then consciously proposed a new model to replace the one he had rejected.

Two aspects of medieval life contributed to his new theory. One was the feudal system in which a lord was responsible to protect his serfs, and the serfs in turn were responsible to honor their lord by giving him what was due to him in terms of services or produce. The other was the penitential system of the church, in which a Christian who confessed his sins might be required by his confessor to render reparations to God for his failure to honor God. The reparations took all sorts of forms from saying prayers to endowing churches or colleges. It is not clear whether Anselm is more indebted to the feudal system or to the penitential system. It is certain that as he developed his view of atonement, he assumed that it was appropriate for a sinner to render reparation or, as he expressed it, satisfaction.

As the title of his book implies, his main objective was to explain why God became man. His thesis was that since man sinned, it is man who should render reparation to God; yet only God is able to render such a reparation; so only one who is both God and man can be the Savior.

This is how the argument of the book runs. Anselm defines sin as failure to render to the honor of God its due.[4] However, God's honor must receive its due, and if man fails to provide it by his obedience, then it will be extracted from man by depriving him of eternal happiness, which is punishment.[5] The only alternative to punishment is for God to receive a satisfactory reparation from man.

As a man Jesus owed God his obedience just as all men do.[6] But he did not owe God his death, since death is required only of sinners. Therefore, by rendering to God his death, Jesus gave more than was required of him, and this could be counted as reparation for man's sins.[7] But could it cover all men's sins? It could, Anselm said, because the murder of Jesus was the murder of one who was God, which was much worse than all other sins combined and was in fact an infinite affront to God's honor. Therefore it followed that Jesus' death itself was an infinite good and could thus conpensate the honor of God for all the sins of all men.[8]

This argument was satisfying and probably even compelling to men in the medieval world. Beginning with a model that arose from the feudal world and the penitential system of the church, it presented the necessity, propriety, and beauty of the incarnation in coherent terms of brilliant clarity.[9] In so doing, it drew upon fundamental realities of life apart from which, it may well have been, men of that day could not understand their existence or that of their world. Quite possibly no model for the atonement ever carried more conviction than this one did to medieval men, sharing as they did virtually every one of its presuppositions.

In Anselm's form, the model is not a part of modern life. The idea of reparation has become questionable today since it seems to be associated with irrational vengeance.[10] It is true that people today still have a largely unconscious desire to see certain kinds of criminals pay for their crimes. For example, many people would want the white minority in South Africa to pay for establishing a social system in which black men are now treated unjustly. But few people will consciously acknowledge that they believe in a general principle of making reparation. In any case, these unconscious desires apply only to certain kinds of crimes and not to all crimes. In short, reparation no longer figures in modern thinking as it did in medieval thought, and this undercuts the credibility of Anselm's model.

My own view of the inadequacy of Anselm for today extends further. I believe that Anselm's theory was too ambitious. Whereas his predecessors like Athanasius had been content to argue for the appropriateness of the incarnation and the cross, Anselm tried to show that the cross was necessary. His title indicates this concern for necessity. I believe it is unwise to seek for a "necessity" for the cross. It is quite possible to affirm and clarify the importance of the cross without speaking of it as necessary. In order to do this, one says simply, "This is what God has done, and this is what it means, and this is how important it is." One need not, in order to affirm the importance of the cross, say, "This is the only way God could have done it."

But these reservations about Anselm's theory should not blind us to his great achievements. In my judgment, his greatest achievement was his successful affirmation of the objectivity of Christ's work. He expressed how, once and for all, whether men know it or not—and many men do not—Christ did something (made reparation to God's honor for man's sin) which provided salvation for men. Though it is true that men must accept Christ's achievement in order to benefit from it, still Christ's achievement does not depend on human response.

No model for atonement which fails to affirm the objectivity of Christ's work can ever be fully satisfactory. Only if Christ did something decisive is there really a Christian gospel at all. Objectivity is essential to the atonement, and Anselm presented it effectively.

John Calvin: Vicarious Punishment

John Calvin, "the most lucid writer in Europe" in the

sixteenth century, provided one of the most concise and vigorous of all Protestant statements concerning atonement, in the last six chapters of Book Two of the *Institutes of the Christian Religion*. Five of the six chapters (12–16) will be dealt with here.

Chapters 12 through 14 present orthodox Christology as it had been defined by the Fourth Ecumenical Council at Chalcedon in A.D. 451. Calvin said that the Son of God, divine by nature, united human nature with his own, thus becoming Jesus of Nazareth, in order to be able to obey God's law on behalf of disobedient men. His obedience was both active, in that he kept God's laws perfectly, and passive, in that he submitted to the humiliation and pain of crucifixion. By his active and passive obedience, Christ rescued disobedient men from the punishment their sins deserved and thus reconciled them to God.

Chapter 15 contains one of the best known of all treatments of Christ's work. It views Christ as Prophet, King, and Priest. As Prophet, Christ taught perfect doctrine, and as King he established a spiritual reign over his subjects. But it is as Priest that Jesus' work is best seen. Calvin said that God is angry at men, and his righteous curse upon sinful men bars their access to him. Jesus offered himself as a sacrifice to appease God's anger, to make satisfaction for sins, and to wash away sin and guilt. God was rendered favorable toward men by Christ's sacrifice.

In chapter 16 Calvin took the same sort of ideas further by putting them into the context which was, I believe, most basic for him. This was neither the master-servant context of chapter 14 nor the sacrificial offering context of chapter 15, but rather the context of the law. No man, Calvin argued, can examine his conscience carefully without recognizing that God's wrath is upon him. As a righteous judge God will not permit his law to be broken without punishment being inflicted. God hates the sinfulness in all men. God punished Jesus for man's sins. This made it possible for God to forego man's punishment and so to forgive men.

Calvin spelled this out by a very attractive procedure. He took the summary of the events of Jesus' life that is given in the Apostles' Creed, and he showed how each event provided specific benefits to Christians.

Thus, because Jesus "suffered under Pontius Pilate," that is in a court of law, it is clear that he stood in the place of guilty men. Just as Pilate pronounced that Jesus was righteous, so God pronounces that Christians are righteous.

By being "crucified," Jesus took the curse which the Bible attaches to that particular kind of execution and so released men from the curse of God's wrath which was upon them.

By "dying," Jesus revealed that he rescues men from death, and he also helped Christians to mortify their members.

By "descending into hell" the Creed meant, not just that Jesus died and not that he preached to people who had died, but that Jesus experienced the torments of hell which are God's punishment of sinners. "Christ was put in the place of evildoers . . . to bear and suffer all the punishments that they ought to have sustained." By sharing the punishment of men in his soul as well as in his body, he rescued both the souls and bodies of sinful men.

What is the basic model in Calvin's theory? It is the model of a substitute who bears the punishment of other men in order that the others may escape their punishment and be forgiven. The context of the model is legal through and through, which is not so surprising in view of the fact that Calvin was educated for a career in law. The basic concept in this legal context is that of substitution, as Paul van Buren made clear in his study of Calvin's doctrine of atonement.[11] And his basic concern was for punishment.

All this is more intelligible if we bear in mind the historical situation within which Calvin wrote. As a reformer, he wanted to correct the failings of Roman Catholicism. Among these the penitential system required that a man who committed a sin and who wanted to avoid God's wrath upon him for that sin, must in effect offer a substitute for his obedience in the form of prayers or pilgrimages or gifts of money to the church. Since these penances were costly, they were painful, and this painful experience amounted to an atonement or appeasement of God's wrath. (In Latin the word for "penance" is derived from the word for punishment.) Most important of all to Calvin, under the penitential system a man never could be sure if he had confessed all his sins, or if he was completely sincere, or if he had offered a really satisfactory sacrifice. Therefore the lives of all Christians were characterized by uncertainty, and this increased in proportion to the intensity of a man's piety.

In order to bring relief to such troubled and unhappy people, Calvin and the other reformers rejected the penitential system. The gospel, they argued, brings confidence and peace, not uncertainty and misery. They went further. Penances were not only unhelpful but they were also unnecessary for the simple reason that obedience has already been provided by Christ, and the punishment of sins that appeases God's wrath has already been experienced by Christ. Since Christ has already paid it all, there is no need for Christians to do penances. They may joyously and confidently trust in Christ's finished work.

Notice that Calvin rejected the idea that the mass and penance were vicarious obediences and punishments that appease God's wrath. He accepted, however, that man can be saved only by vicarious obedience and punishment, and he joyously proclaimed that Jesus had done all that was required.

Among Protestants, Calvin's theory of atonement has been perhaps the most influential one developed since the close of the New Testament. Our evaluation of it will deal with three distinct factors. They are the general idea of substitution, the general idea of punishment, and the particular idea of substitutionary punishment.

1. The general idea of substitution is fundamentally a good idea. It is noble for one person to accept painful experiences on behalf of another person he loves in order to do for that other person things that he cannot do for himself.

Of course, like any good idea, it can become perverse. For example, it could be ineffectual and unhealthy to become a substitute for another for no purpose. And it is immoral to substitute for another if that means preventing him from doing his best. But Calvin did not fall into either of these errors. He saw Christ as man's substitute in a very positive way.

2. The general idea of punishment is much more complicated. It is not that Calvin's view is obscure—here, as usual, he is a model of clarity: men have sinned; God punishes sin; Jesus accepted God's punishment of sin; so men do not have to do penance or otherwise suffer punishment for their sin. "The Lawgiver will not punish the same sins twice." [12] The problem with Calvin's view of punishment is his idea that within God there is a tension between love and righteousness. He felt that though in love God wanted to save men, in righteousness he was required to punish all sins. Only when the demands of righteousness had been met, by punishing Jesus as a substitute for men, was God in a position to forgive. But there is no such tension in God's love. Salvation

is a function both of love and of righteousness, and so is punishment.

We can make this clearer by distinguishing three positions. First, there is the idea that Christ purchased God's love by his sacrifice. Calvin specifically rejected this. Second, there is the idea that in God, love and righteousness are in tension, love wanting to forgive men and righteousness requiring their punishment. This is Calvin's position, and he saw the cross as meeting the requirements of justice that punishment be inflicted, yet allowing love to provide forgiveness. Third, there is the position that I am suggesting, that love and righteousness both are effective in punishment, and they are both involved in divine forgiveness.

3. What often misleads men about substitutionary punishment is their understanding of what punishment is. It is not just pain. Men may experience pain, even the pain that is ordinarily associated with punishment of a particular crime, without being punished by God for that crime. That is what happened to Jesus. Men punished him for alleged crimes, probably blasphemy and revolution, but God, who knew he was righteous, did not disapprove of him at all; he approved of him. To put it another way, Jesus experienced the pain which a man might feel if he were being punished by God for great sins, but he was not punished by God.

We have concluded that substitution is a moral idea and that Jesus stood in man's place. We also concluded that punishment is a moral idea. We also acknowledge that what Jesus experienced might easily be interpreted as divine punishment if someone else experienced it. But we saw no reason to believe as Calvin did that the Father punished Jesus. Instead of disapproving of Jesus, which is what punishment is, God approved of him, as the resurrection eloquently testified.

Although we cannot accept Calvin's view of substitutionary punishment, we can understand how he arrived at it. He believed that God determines by his will what is right and wrong. If he determined that all sin must be punished and that one man could bear the punishment of others, that would make it so. Therefore, given Calvin's presuppositions about God's sovereignty, the concept of vicarious punishment was an appropriate way to understand Christ's death.

Men today do not ordinarily hold this view of God as simply willing right and wrong, and so they cannot believe that vicarious punishment is either meaningful or moral. No illustration can be given, so far as I can tell, which makes vicarious punishment morally credible to men today. The stories of one soldier punished for another, a child punished for his brother, a man punished for his friend, may be morally praiseworthy from the point of view of the substitute, but they never are acceptable from the point of view of the punisher. It always seems morally outrageous that any judge would require a substitute. However noble the substitute's act might be, the judge's act seems despicable.

The single exception to this concerns punishment in the form of a monetary fine. In such cases, one person is permitted to pay the fine for another person. It does not seem morally wrong for a judge to require, for example, a youth to pay a fine and then to accept payment of the fine from the youth's father. This might be made to serve as a model for Christ's work, and an argument can be made for the appropriateness of financial words in describing atonement. However, there is one problem, and it is that no judge in a Western court today would allow for substitutionary incarceration. Further, no judge would permit one man's execution in place of another, let alone demand such a substitution. And what Christ gave was precisely his life. To demand death as a substitutionary punishment is simply morally reprehensible.

Calvin's model works if one shares his presuppositions about God's sovereignty. It does not work if one does not, and almost no one today does. A model ought to explain the cross, including the moral achievement of Christ. If it raises moral doubts about the cross, it is an unsuitable model.

John McLeod Campbell: Vicarious Repentance

John McLeod Campbell was a nineteenth-century Scottish pastor whose reputation as a theologian rests on a single book, *The Nature of the Atonement and Its Relation to Remission of Sins and Eternal Life.* The book reveals the author's patient meditation on Jesus and his cross. Campbell wrote in dialogue with the Calvinism which was his heritage. He held certain presuppositions in common with Calvinism, one of which is that Christ's mediating work can be understood only on the basis of his being both divine and human.[13] Another idea he held along with Calvinists was that the atoning work of Christ must be an objective achievement, not simply a revelation of God's love but an act of love seen to be effective.[14] He also argued that this objectivity is emphasized if we can say why the cross was necessary for man's salvation,[15] though as we shall see, he understood the necessity differently than the Calvinists.

He also regarded some features of Calvinism as objectionable. He said that the cross is an expression of God's love, not a means of obtaining it for sinners.[16] He regarded the idea that God punished Christ for man's sins as a legal fiction which is a false and immoral idea.[17] God could never be truly revealed in such an arbitrary act.[18] Nevertheless, he agreed with Calvin that God's forgiveness is not indulgence. Men are sinners, God does punish sin, and forgiveness is a reality—Campbell felt all this was essential to understanding the cross.

Campbell felt that Calvinism regarded God's attributes as in conflict when it taught that as love God forgives and as righteous he condemns.[19] The truth is rather that righteousness also is concerned with salvation which, after all, is making men righteous.[20] And even though he loves, God must condemn men since it is only by rejecting their rebellion that he really supports their welfare.[21] Love and righteousness are united, therefore, because God's condemnation of sin and his concern for man's welfare are two aspects of the same reality.

Campbell saw Calvinism in his own day as having developed into two strains. One tradition taught that Christ died only for the elect, a position which Campbell rejected as untrue to the gospel.[22] The other tradition saw Christ's death as an act of rectoral justice, God having punished Christ in order to prove to men that God is genuinely committed to righteousness and that his leniency should never be presumed upon. Campbell rejected this view as immoral, since punishment is only appropriate when it is deserved.[23]

But it is not in these details that Campbell most decisively departed from his heritage. He changed the entire idea of atonement by using a model taken from a family setting rather than one taken from a legal setting. He insisted that the family setting is more basic than the legal,[24] that it is better to think of God as Father than as Judge,[25] and that the fundamental meaning of salvation is sonship rather than justification.[26]

Few people today would argue with this emphasis on the personal, at least in principle. But it was a revolutionary idea in 1856. And it created a difficulty for Campbell. How would he be able to express, in a family setting, the objective achievement of the cross? What had Jesus accomplished, once for all, that provided forgiveness for sinners? Campbell had an answer to that question that was as ingenious as it was bold. He felt that what Jesus did was to identify with sinful man in such a way that he could put himself in their place before God, even with regard to sin. In other words, Jesus acted as a sinner ought to act when God condemns his sin—he confessed the sinfulness of sin and the righteousness of judgment. He gave "a perfect Amen in humanity to the judgment of God on the sin of man." [27] He experienced a sense of and adopted an attitude of perfect repentance which was an atoning sacrifice because repentance is the one thing to which God responds with unqualified forgiveness.

Campbell felt that the only acceptable atonement is genuine repentance. But the trouble is that men cannot really repent precisely because they *are* sinners.[28] So Christ did it for men. He made a confession of human sin as man's brother, not as a legal stand-in.[29] He made it quite naturally, as a continuation of his loving identification with sinners.[30] What was atoning about it was, not Christ's sufferings, but his love and holiness responding, as they must in his circumstances, to God's holiness and love.[31]

The obvious retort to Campbell's view is that the New Testament does not present Christ as repenting for men's sins. Campbell doubtless felt this, and he did his best to fill in the gap. He drew upon the prayers of Christ for men,[32] upon Christ's intercession for men following his ascension into heaven,[33] upon Christ's identification with sinners by his earthly ministry, and upon Christ's prayer for forgiveness for his executioners.[34] He also argued that it was inevitable that a good man would feel a sense of shame at the rebellion of his fellows. Campbell contrasted his view with the artificial role of Christ as suffering punishment at God's hand.

Christ's work was natural, expiatory, and vicarious, but it was not punishment.

In my judgment, the strength of Campbell's theory was its use of a model from a family setting. He was surely right to insist that we can best understand the cross if we liken it to the response of a loving but conscientious father to his child's rebellion. But is that response one of confession of the child's sins? Of vicarious repentance? I do not believe that it is. Though we agree that one can feel a sense of vicarious shame for the sin of another, it is difficult to see that very much is achieved by this, taken by itself. Why would God forgive men because Christ felt full repentance? It is true that man cannot completely, truly repent—as Campbell says—but if forgiveness is the appropriate response to repentance, then it is appropriate to forgive the repentant rather than the unrepentant. It is not the quality or fullness of repentance that matters but the fact that it represents an opportunity for God to enter into a man's life and to begin his work. That can happen, however, only if a man repents for his own sins. Vicarious repentance could, it seems to me, contribute nothing to it at all.

So I feel that Campbell's thesis fails. This leaves us with this dilemma: If like him we feel that the best models for the cross are those taken from interpersonal life, how are we to understand the objectivity of Christ's work?

P. T. Forsyth: Vicarious Obedience

P. T. Forsyth was a Congregational educator who moved from a liberal theology to a modified traditional position. He felt that what theology needed early in the twentieth century was for dogma to be moralized.[35] What he meant by moralizing dogma can be expressed in several ways, one of which is that the basic models for theological explanation should be taken, not from legal or metaphysical contexts, but from the context of the moral relationships between persons. He felt that if this procedure were followed it would result in a transformation of theology. He acknowledged that the legal context had been of value, especially in reminding men of the holiness of God. That moral core of theology, which had largely been forfeited by liberalism, needed to be preserved, but that could be done better in a personal context than in the legal; the legal context is not large enough to contain the gospel.[36]

Forsyth wrote two books about the atonement; in fact, all his books were about Christ's work, whatever his topic happened to be. Therefore it is difficult to decide which of the many models he employed is most fundamental to him. In addition, his writing is highly rhetorical, which makes the choice even more difficult. Nevertheless, in view of his concern for moral, personal relationships, the most fundamental thing for Forsyth seems to have been the idea of Christ's obedience to the Father. In fact, Forsyth took great pains to say that the really important thing about Jesus' sacrifice was not the blood, the suffering, the death, or the cross, but rather his obedience which led up to these things.[37]

The obedience of Christ should be understood as objective, Forsyth argued. By this he meant that it was an historical act which cannot be repeated, in contrast to a word which can. "Something had to be *done*—judging or saving. Revelation alone is inadequate.[38]

Christ's obedience was objective in another sense also. It was an act done by God, not by men. "The real meaning of an objective atonement is that God himself made the complete sacrifice." In fact, only God could have done this work: "Everything turns upon this—whether Christ was a created being, however grand, or whether He was of incarnate Godhead." [39]

Even though it was God in Christ who was perfectly obedient, his work is not objective in the sense of being done
apart from men, over their heads. "The great transaction was
done for the race. But objective as it was, gift as it was from
pure grace, it was so in its initiative rather than in its
method."[40] We shall return later to the question of how men
were involved in Christ's sacrifice.

It was very important to Forsyth that Christ's obedience
was a justification of God. God could only justify men before
himself by justifying himself before men.[41] This means more
than that men see God to be righteous. It means also that God
acted in Christ in such a way that righteousness was established and secured in the world. It means that God's conscience has been met in the way he has acted: "His conscience
had to be pacified as well as His heart indulged." [42] God is
holy; he acts in holy ways; in Christ he acted so that his
holiness was clear to men.

We can see the justification of God only if we admit that
Christ's death was a *judgment,* which is a better word than
penalty, which Forsyth allowed, or *punishment,* which he
rejected.[43] God does not ignore sin. He judges it. This is seen
in Christ. It is not that the Father punished the Son, which is
untrue, or that Jesus was punished directly at all.[44] But he
did sustain the kind of experience which is appropriate for
sinners. "There is a penalty and curse for sin; and Christ
consented to enter that region. Christ entered voluntarily
into the pain and horror which is sin's penalty from God." [45]
"The divine judgment of sin is real and effective. That is, it
fell where it was perfectly understood, owned, and
praised." [46] By this obedience of judgment Christ justified
God. But there is more, for God's holy judgment of sin,
having once been made in a way that sustained his holiness,

is finished. "I have a way of putting it that startles some of my friends. The last judgment is past. It took place on Christ's cross." [47]

Christ's holy obedience, by which he justified God's holiness, can be understood in two ways. "On the one hand it was God offering, and on the other hand it was man confessing." [48] It was a sacrifice precisely because Christ was obedient, not merely unto death, but unto judgment. "He turned the penalty he endured into a sacrifice he offered." [49] Thus he transformed the Old Testament symbolism of the self-surrender of a worshiper in offering his sacrifice into a great moral reality for the world. [50]

Of all his ways of expressing Christ's obedience, Forsyth seems to have favored the idea of confession. Jesus confessed God's holiness by his entire obedient life, and consummated his confession by his obedient death. His obedience was an "Amen" coming from within the human race to affirm God's holiness in all things, even in the difficult thing, namely, divine judgment.

So far we have said that Forsyth used obedience as his basic model for Christ's work, that this is understood in the context of moral relationships, that it is objective in that it is God's completed act in history, that it justified God by affirming his holiness, and that it is both a sacrifice God made and a confession man made. Now it is time to see how all this benefits man.

Forsyth spoke of a threefold cord of the cross. By his obedience unto judgment Jesus won a final victory over evil, he regenerated evil men to good men, and he satisfied the demands of the holy God for holiness.[51] The victory over evil and the regeneration of sinners into good men are really two expressions of the same reality.[52] That is, redemption understood positively is the transformation of evil men into good men, and negatively it is release from the powers of evil. Also, it is holiness, in Christ but also in men, that satisfies God. We must examine these three aspects of Christ's work more closely.

Of the three, only the idea of victory is at all clear. By this Forsyth meant that Christ has somehow released men from sin's bondage. He "broke the power of evil by living it down." [53]

Sanctification is more complex. It rests on Forsyth's conviction that there is a moral unity of Christ and the human race. It is not a natural unity; Christ had to establish a special unity by his identification with men.[54] This solidarity of Christ and the race means that his obedience contains men's obedience, as a cause contains the effect.[55] His sacrifice was man's sacrifice; his confession, man's. He represented the race as a federal head.[56] His cross is itself the source of the new life in men. Christ "created that holiness in us by living it in" at the cross.[57] His union with us could not make him a sinner for he was obedient, but it can make men righteous, and it did so by his obedience.

It is by this holiness, of Christ's obedience which is also man's, that God is satisfied, for nothing but holiness ever could have satisfied God. Because God is satisfied, his treatment of men changed at the cross. He always felt love for men, but love is capable of intense anger, and that anger characterized the holy God's treatment of men until he was satisfied by Christ's holiness.[58] Jesus did not placate the Father.[59] Nor was there a strife between God's love and his holiness. Rather, as loving and holy he judged men; now that his judgment is past, Christ having been obedient unto judgment, God treats men with acceptance, not judgment. That, in turn, creates faith in men, and their faith leads to their sanctification, the working out in their lives of the work

Christ did for them, and their liberation from sin.

It is difficult to appraise Forsyth's theory because it is obscure. Its obscurity arises, I believe, from the setting and model he used. What exactly did he mean by "moral"? It is clear that he did not mean, for example, metaphysical. But what did he mean? The problem is that the moral setting as such does not exist. It is halfway between two clear settings, the legal and the personal, but it does not exist on its own. So Forsyth was in effect shifting back and forth between two models, which naturally led to obscurity.

He was unclear, for example, when he said that God needed to establish his holiness in the sense of accepting judgment or proving to men that he does judge sin. All I think that we can meaningfully say is that, as holy, God acts righteously, and he has acted in Christ.

Further, I cannot accept Forsyth's idea of solidarity. It is true that Jesus was a man, one of the human race. But as close as one person may be to others, we should not lose the distinction between persons. We should understand Christ's work as his own, and then ask how men are related to it, rather than say that men were really there at the cross, they were obedient, they were judged. There is a place in Christian piety for affirming Christ's identification with men and man's life with him. This may be expressed by saying men are in him as a branch is in a vine or a member in a body. There is even room for mystical talk about union with Christ and for language about substitution, representation, identification, and sympathy. But we must stop short of saying, "I was Christ, obedient unto judgment." It was Forsyth's failure to move entirely out of the legal setting into the personal setting that led him into this confusion of Christ and Christians.

Without this view of solidarity, Forsyth is left saying that

Christ obeyed God in man's place. Obviously this will not do. He did obey God, and what he did is to man's eternal benefit. But it was not obedience instead of men; rather it was obedience so that men could be liberated for obedience. The model of vicarious obedience will not do.

On the other hand, Forsyth's work is full of suggestive ideas that can be developed in ways that avoid his problems. Here are four: (1) that the cross was indispensable and crucial; (2) that atonement was an act, not just a word; (3) that it was objective but not as traditionally thought before God (and I would add, not as Forsyth thought, because it was by God—there is another sense of objectivity which he did not suggest); (4) that Christ did not merely prepare for the reconciliation of God and man, he actually reconciled them. "He was not making it possible, he was doing it." [60]   We hope to incorporate all of these ideas in our theory of atonement.

Hastings Rashdall: Moral Influence

Although Hastings Rashdall's book *The Idea of the Atonement in Christian Theology* was not published until 1920, it contained his Bampton Lectures delivered at Oxford in 1915, which is more or less the end of the period in which liberal Protestantism dominated European theology. Rashdall's book is a classic statement of the liberal view of the atonement.

In this book we are looking for a link that unites the story of Christ at Calvary with the experience Christians today have of being forgiven. Rashdall felt that there was no such connection. He had two reasons for this. First, forgiveness is something which God does freely. There are no conditions he must fulfill in order to be able to forgive men. In fact, God is obligated to forgive men whenever they repent of their sin. He wrote: "That sin ought to be forgiven when there is sincere repentance is a truth which, like all ultimate ethical truths, must be accepted simply because it is self-evident." [61] The cross of Jesus has nothing to do with forgiveness. Second, Rashdall's supreme concern was to establish a connection, not between the cross and forgiveness, but between the cross and the moral transformation of a sinner into a righteous man. Because moral transformation was his great concern, Rashdall ignored, when he did not disavow, a connection between the cross and forgiveness.

Rashdall believed that Jesus transforms men's character by his lofty moral teaching, by his exemplary life, and by his concern for men's welfare. Christ was so committed to his mission to teach that he would die rather than abstain from teaching. That is what he did, of course, and men who reflect upon that sacrifice are moved with gratitude to the Father for Jesus and his ministry. That gratitude is the source of their moral transformation. Men's love is awakened by God's love revealed in Jesus and particularly in his unselfish death.[62]

Jesus was not the only revelation of God's love, of course. Whenever human beings care enough for one another to act unselfishly, that is a revelation of God's love. But Jesus stands at the summit of revelation because his life was so perfect and his suffering so intense.[63]

This view of atonement, argued Rashdall, is simple and sufficient. It is simple because it is the most natural thing in the world for one person to influence another, and that is what Jesus has done to an absolute degree.[64] And it is sufficient to explain the transformation of men. The efficacy of Christ's death is its power to effect ethical change in the lives of those who meditate upon him.[65] After all, if Christ by his revelation of God through an exemplary life and teaching and death can make men good, what more could anyone ask for?

Rashdall said that Christ revealed not only God's love but also God's suffering. God loves men, and in view of the fact that they are sinners and that they experience pain, the inescapable conclusion is that God suffers with them, sympathetically. Not that Christ's sufferings were actually God's sufferings—to say that would be to confuse Jesus and God and tend toward pantheism—but Christ's sufferings do mean that God, whose character is like Christ's, experiences suffering.[66]

Rashdall summarized his view by rephrasing a statement in Acts: "There is none other ideal given among men by which we may be saved except the moral ideal which Christ taught by His words and illustrated by His life and death of love: and there is none other help so great in the attainment of that ideal as the belief in God as He has been supremely revealed in Him who so taught and lived and died." [67]

Since this view is so different from any other dealt with in this book, we may wonder how Rashdall tried to justify it. He did so in terms of the Bible and of church history, his discussions of which occupied seven of his eight chapters.

Jesus, said Rashdall, taught that forgiveness is granted to those who repent. He said nothing about his own death as a condition of divine forgiveness. Rashdall admits that two sayings of Jesus do seem to contradict his view, the ransom saying (Mark 10:45) and the words of the institution of the Lord's Supper. Rashdall argued that the ransom saying is not authentic, but even if it were, it says nothing about forgiveness. In the words spoken at the Supper, the expression concerning forgiveness is a latter addition; but even if it were not, its reference is to the new covenant of Jeremiah 31 and not to a sacrificial offering.

To his great credit, Rashdall admitted that Paul and the book of Hebrews taught doctrines of atonement which dif-

fered from his own, Paul's a forensic one and Hebrews' a
sacrificial one. Rashdall frankly confessed that he did not
accept their views.

But, he argued, there are two strands in Paul's thought.[68]
The fundamental one expresses his experience of being morally influenced by the cross and thus transformed. The other
is an extraneous one forced on early Christians by their
situation. They believed in Jesus, yet Jesus had died. How
could they explain that fact? As Jews, they were forced to
explain it in terms of the Old Testament. It is for that reason
that they employed metaphors of sacrifice and expiation.
These we can "put aside" since they rest "upon a misin-
terpretation of Jewish prophecy." [69] We are then left with the
pure teaching that God's love kindles a man's response and
changes his life.

Rashdall's thesis was simple, as he said. One way to grasp
what he meant is to observe his criticism of the more traditional views of atonement. These are scattered throughout
his book, but may be summarized as follows.

First, the idea of an eternal hell is immoral. If God is like
Christ, then he would not torment people eternally.[70] This
may not lead to universalism, but it does mean that the view
of atonement which sees Christ as rescuing men from hell is
incorrect.

Second, the idea of satisfaction is immoral.[71] God's love,
forgiveness, and salvation do not have to be purchased.
Whether the satisfaction is to God's honor, a payment under
civil law which is Anselm's view, or to God's justice, a
punishment under criminal law which was Calvin's view, it
is immoral. Rashdall rejected the entire concept of satisfaction. In fact, any sort of transaction at all indicated a faulty
view of the Trinity.[72]

Third, the idea that Christ was somehow corporate humanity is a false idea, "the old bastard Platonism." [73] This idea, which appeared as we saw in Athanasius and Forsyth, has been a major constituent of many views of atonement. Rashdall avoided it, preferring to be quite clear on the fact that Jesus was Jesus and men are men, and no confusing of that distinction is allowed.

Fourth, Rashdall believed that repentance is the only condition for forgiveness, and to make faith in Christ, and especially faith in the cross of Christ, a condition of forgiveness is arbitrary and therefore immoral. To do so is more than an addition to the teaching of Jesus, which might be permissible. It is a contradiction of it and must be abandoned.[74]

Fifth, traditional views of atonement isolate Christ's death from his life and especially from his teaching.[75] This is tragic, said Rashdall. In all his life, teaching, and death, Christ was doing a single saving work for man—showing man the moral way of life and providing a motivation for living it. To separate Christ's death from the rest of his work is arbitrary and distorts the meaning of everything.

How are we to appraise Rashdall's view? It was, as he said, a simple model. I would add that it is a model that carries conviction: Jesus does transform men into better men by the example and inspiration of his life and death. Further, it was right of Rashdall to isolate and omit the morally offensive elements in some theories of atonement. Further, Rashdall was right to insist that God is concerned not only to forgive men but also to transform them into good men. Any view of atonement which can say nothing about how men become good must be rejected. Rashdall was right that the meaning of the cross is not to be found between the Father and the Son but is all a work of God. Rashdall was also right to reject the view that what Christ did he did as corporate man. Whatever value there may be in speaking of the union of the

Christian with Christ, and of Christ's acting on behalf of all the race, still it was God in Christ who acted in and experienced the cross, and not mankind. This salvation was God's work. There should be no confusion of Christ and man.

So Rashdall achieved many helpful things. Unfortunately, his own view is open to serious question. For one thing, he distorted Jesus' teaching about the cross. Jesus said some things which Rashdall couldn't accept; so he tried to read them out. And Rashdall's distinction between the fundamental teaching of Paul and others about Christ's moral influence, resting in their experience, and their extraneous ideas resting only on misunderstandings of the Old Testament, simply will not do for this reason: The distinctive New Testament experience, as recorded in Acts and reflected in the Epistles, is precisely the one which Rashdall denies, namely, that Christians are those who have received forgiveness through the blood of Christ. What Rashdall has omitted is not a gloss on Christian experience, as he thought, but the fundamental experience itself—forgiveness through the sacrifice of Christ. This prevents Rashdall from ever raising a really important question—what is the relationship between forgiveness and the transformation of character?

Furthermore, as incredible as it may seem, Rashdall makes forgiveness a very easy thing for God to do. When he speaks of God suffering, Rashdall means that God feels sympathy for suffering man. But God's forgiveness, so far as Rashdall indicates, costs God nothing. It is true that Jesus died, and this assists man's moral transformation. According to Rashdall, however, this contributed nothing to forgiveness, which is apparently effortless on God's part.

Finally, as a consequence of this problem, Rashdall knows nothing of a victory at the cross. Jesus begins to achieve something worthwhile for men only when they are influenced by his action. Until then, his death achieves nothing—no liberation, no redemption, no triumph. It was a noble act but not an effective one, taken alone. Is this all that can be said of Jesus' death? I think not.

Gustaf Aulen: Vicarious Victor

It is an indication of the importance of Gustaf Aulen's *Christus Victor* that it was translated into English within a year of its original publication in Swedish in 1930. It is a small book with a large, bold thesis, which is that the history of the doctrine of the atonement has always been misrepresented because one major theory of atonement has not been understood by the historians. The usual history of the doctrine speaks of a continuing conflict between two theories, the objective view associated with Anselm and the subjective view associated with Abelard and with many modern exponents like Hastings Rashdall.[76] The third view which is ignored in this scheme is the one which portrays Christ as struggling against evil forces and, by the cross, defeating them, thus liberating men who had been slaves to them. "Its central theme is the idea of the Atonement as a Divine conflict and victory; Christ—*Christus Victor*—fights against and triumphs over the evil powers of the world, the 'tyrants' under which mankind is in bondage and suffering, and in Him God reconciles the world to Himself." [77] A proper history of the doctrine would place this view alongside of and as an alternative to the subjective and objective views.

Aulen describes the victor view as dramatic, for the obvious reason that it speaks of a drama of redemption rather than of a rationale for redemption. The drama occurs against a background that is dualistic, with God locked in combat against the forces of evil. These forces are variously described by proponents of the victor view, and their constituents include sin, death, wrath, the law, and the devil.

Aulen argued that the victor view is the classic one because it was dominant in the New Testament, the Fathers,
and Luther. In the New Testament, Jesus was portrayed as an
exorcist who defeated the demons by healing and the devil
and death by his sacrifice.[78] Paul stressed the cosmic dimension of Jesus' victory over demonic principalities and powers.[79] The Fathers employed graphic and even grotesque
images to assert Christ's victory over the devil. For example,
Gregory of Nyssa compared the devil to a fish caught on the
hook of Jesus' deity which was concealed in the bait of his
humanity, and Augustine compared the cross to a mousetrap
which snared the devil.[80] The victor idea lost its dominant
position to the legalistic view of Anselm, said Aulen, but it
was reasserted with great power by Luther.[81] Aulen argued
that in these writers and others it is an error to assume that
ideas like ransom, debt, punishment, and sacrifice belong
within the Latin, legal tradition.[82] They often belong rather
in the classic dramatic view where they indicate, not a satisfaction of legal requirements of justice, but a victory Christ
won over the enemies of mankind.

Aulen refused to call the classic view a theory. It is a
theme or a motif rather than a rounded and finished doctrine.[83] It cannot become a rational doctrine because it contains irreconcilable paradoxes. The most important of these
arises from the fact that the tyrants which Christ defeated are
themselves subject to God and therefore executants of his
will. This means that in overcoming them Christ was simul-
taneously reconciling God to man.[84] It is not possible to put
these two concepts together rationally.[85] That is, however,
not a weakness but a strength of the classic view, Aulen
argued, since "it may be doubted, however, whether this
demand for rational clearness represents the highest

theological wisdom." [86] It is better to retain the paradoxes. Since only the classic view is willing to do that, it is superior to the others and should replace them. The subjective view is in any case far too humanistic,[87] and the Latin view of Anselm, though it represents God as planning the atonement, still asserts that it was as a man that Christ made satisfaction to God for sins. In other words, only the classic view presented the atonement as a work of God from beginning to end. Therein lies its superiority.

Aulen has suggested a very definite model for the atonement, one whose background and assumptions are evident. Its greatest strengths are that it portrays the universality of Christ's work and its victorious character. If affirms that Christ died not only to forgive men of sins for which they are responsible but also to liberate them from the powers of evil for which they are not responsible but which have nevertheless entrapped men and are destroying them. In other words, it shows Christ dealing with the problem of evil generally as well as with the sins of individuals.

Further, it asserts, in a way that was lacking, for example, in Rashdall's model, the victorious quality of Christ's sacrifice, apart from which it is difficult to see what resources a Christian would have for wrestling with the evil in the world. What hope, joy, or enthusiasm could there be in Christ's death seen only as a martyrdom, however noble?

So Aulen's view, understood as qualifying Christ's death as cosmic and victorious, makes an important contribution to the doctrine of the atonement. However, as an explanation of atonement it fails for the simple reason that it is not intelligible. This is true partly because of the paradoxes it contains, but, more than that, it is not intelligible because we cannot understand what it means to say that Christ destroyed evil forces. How does one destroy evil forces? To make the victor motif into a model of atonement, rather than just a qualifier of some other basic model, would require that one put some meaning into the words "destroy evil forces."

Several attempts have been made to do this, though not by Aulen, who admitted frankly that if we take the view literally it can be absurd.[88] To make the evil forces objective it has been suggested that they are the dehumanizing elements in social life or the idols which modern men worship just as really as first-century men worshiped their false gods.[89] An alternative move is to regard the cross as evidence that one day God will overcome death, pain, and so on.[90] A more subjective interpretation is that Christ's victory over sin means that he freed men from guilt feelings; his victory over law means he freed men from the tyranny of moralism and legalism, and so on.

Although these are useful heuristic enterprises, they do not render the idea of victory a basic model for the meaning of Christ's death, and ironically they do not really provide what the classic view ought best to provide, which is a sense of the cosmic dimension of Christ's redemption and of the victorious consequences of his death. It is better to select a basic model from human experience for understanding Christ's death, one in which the victorious element will be clear, and then show how the effects of that victory fan out to overcome all the kinds of tyranny to which human beings are subject. This ought to be done as much as possible in positive rather than negative terms, saying what men are liberated unto as well as what they are liberated from, a matter concerning which Aulen remained vague. [91]

Don S. Browning: Psychotherapy

In Don Browning's book *Atonement and Psychotherapy* we encounter for the first time a model for the atonement which makes no claim at all to have originated in the New Testament.[92] Browning believed that the truth about the atonement is given in the New Testament, but modern analogies for the cross can be employed to clarify and confirm that truth.

The model Browning used for the cross is the work of psychologists who practice the client-centered therapy of Carl Rogers.[93] In client-centered therapy, the therapist's work consists of several elements. One is empathy, in which the therapist attempts to feel his client's feelings along with him. Though it is a passive matter, it is also active because it achieves important results. We must learn "what psychotherapy has to tell us about the efficacy of the passive element in any act of healing."[94] Feeling along with and for another person is a very costly experience for the therapist.[95] It is a vicarious experience, and, to the extent that the feelings of the client are self-condemnation, it is actually an experience of penal suffering.[96]

Along with empathy for the client's pain, the therapist also feels the client's hostility toward the therapist.[97] This hostility occurs because the route of healing that the client is following threatens him even as it heals him. Naturally he directs the hostility which his anxiety creates toward the therapist.

Along with empathy and the acceptance of hostility, the therapist is accepting his client unconditionally.[98] This does not mean that he is permissively approving all of the client's actions, but it does mean that he is for the client, that he accepts him as a person, and that he relates to the client with positive regard.

The basic conviction of client-centered therapy is that when a therapist relates to a client in this way, healing is inevitable. Browning's conviction is that this is the best analogy for the way in which God relates to men. He is convinced that because God feels empathetically with broken men, accepts their hostility, and treats them with unconditional positive regard, they will be healed.

What is the role of Christ in the divine healing procedure? Christ is a witness to the fact that God relates to men in this therapeutic way.[99] According to Browning, "the event of Jesus Christ manifests a reality that is present already. The event of Jesus Christ in no way reconstitutes our relationship to God or changes God himself." [100] Christ's manifestation of God's therapeutic empathy and positive regard is essential to the healing process. If men were not made aware that God relates to them in this healing way, then the healing would not occur, just as a client can benefit from his therapist's work only if he is aware of it. So Jesus, in bearing witness to God's eternal healing work, is making that work effective in men's lives; he is the dynamic presentation of the eternal atonement.[101]

The great achievement of Browning's book is its candid employment of a nonbiblical model which convincingly and clearly conveys an explanation of Christ's work. This model is taken from the setting of interpersonal relationships rather than of law. I believe that this is the best background for models of atonement today, because I feel that the divine-human relationship is like nothing else so much as it is like human interpersonal relationships. I also think Browning was wise to specify the kind of interpersonal relationship he meant. Often theologians leave us unsure whether they are thinking of parent-child, teacher-student, husband-wife, or friend-friend relationships. Browning was clearly thinking of a therapist-client relationship. This specific model is very effective for presenting the healing of human emotional brokenness. And I believe that Browning is right to point out that healing involves costly suffering on God's part. The passive experience of suffering can achieve real results.

The weakness of the psychotherapeutic model is that it cannot represent the healing of sin understood as guilt. In other words, the client has done wrong, but he has not done wrong to the therapist. If he had, their relationship would be altered. The therapist feels the client's self-condemnation, and even his hostility which results from the anxiety accompanying the therapy, but that is not exactly the same thing as feeling sinned against. And it is just this that characterizes God's relationship with man—men have sinned against God, and God has experienced what it is to be sinned against. What is needed is a model which includes this particular aspect of the divine-human relationship. And perhaps, when one is found, it will also have a place in it for seeing Christ's historical work, not only as an example of an eternal healing act of God as Browning said, but as itself the actual achievement of that healing.

NOTES

[1] The full title is On the Incarnation of the Word and His Manifestation to Us through the Body.

[2] Athanasius, The Incarnation, par. 54.

[3] Ibid., par. 9.

[4] Anselm, Why God Became Man, I, 6.

[5] Ibid., 14.   [6] Anselm, II, 11.

[7] Ibid., 18.   [8] Ibid., 14.

[10] The most convincing modern theory of atonement using reparation known to me is that of K. E. Kirk, "The Atonement" in Essays Catholic and Critical, ed. E. G. Selwyn (London: SPCK, 1926).

[11] Paul van Buren, Christ in Our Place (Edinburgh: Oliver and Boyd, 1957).

[12] T. H. L. Parker, John Calvin (London: J. M. Dent and Sons, Ltd., 1975), p. 38.

[13] John McLeod Campbell, *The Nature of the Atonement and Its Relation to Remission of Sins and Eternal Life* (Cambridge: Macmillan and Co., 1856), pp. 26, 375–376.

[14] Ibid., p. 26.   [15] Ibid., p. 185.

[16] Ibid., p. 19. The view that the cross purchased God's love had been denied by Calvin himself but was held by some of his successors.

[17] Ibid., p. 78.   [18] Ibid., p. 187.

[19] Ibid., pp. 29–30, 62.   [20] Ibid., p. 30.

[21] Ibid., p. 306.   [22] Ibid., p. 59.

[23] Ibid., p. 80.   [24] Ibid., pp. 72, 211.

[25] Ibid., p. 104.   [26] Ibid., p. 345.

[27] Ibid., p. 134.   [28] Ibid., p. 143.

[29] Ibid., p. 145.   [30] Ibid., p. 157.

[31] Ibid., pp. 114–115.   [32] Ibid., pp. 229–231.

[33] Ibid., Chapter Nine.   [34] Ibid., p. 286.

[35] P. T. Forsyth, *The Work of Christ* (London: Hodder and Stoughton, 1910), p. 228.

[36] Ibid., p. 187.

[37] Ibid., p. 157. See also P. T. Forsyth, *The Cruciality of the Cross* (London: Independent Press Ltd., 1909), pp. 85–104.

[38] Ibid., *The Work of Christ*, p. 57.

[39] Ibid., pp. 158–159.   [40] Ibid., p. 226.

[41] Ibid., p. 136.   [42] Ibid., p. 167.

[43] Ibid., p. 182.   [44] Ibid., p. 146.

[45] Ibid., p. 147.   [46] Ibid., p. 83.

[47] Ibid., p. 160.   [48] Ibid., p. 148.

[49] Ibid., p. 163.   [50] Ibid., p. 164.

[51] Ibid., p. 199ff.   [52] Ibid., p. 202.

[53] Ibid., p. 209.   [54] Ibid., p. 215.

[55] Ibid., p. 188.   [56] Ibid., p. 172.

[57] Ibid., p. 209.   [58] Ibid., pp. 104–105.

[59] Ibid., p. 101.   [60] Ibid., p. 182.

[61] Hastings Rashdall, *The Idea of the Atonement in Christian Theology* (London: Macmillan and Co., Ltd., 1920), p. 49.

[62] Ibid., p. 463.

[63] Ibid., p. 448.   [64] Ibid., p. 357.

[65] Ibid., p. 437.   [66] Ibid., pp. 452–454.

[67] Ibid., p. 463.   [68] Ibid., pp. 148, 160.

[69] Ibid., pp. 436–347.   [70] Ibid., p. 458.

[71] Ibid., p. 423.   [72] Ibid., p. 445.

[73] Ibid., pp. 358, 423–425.   [74] Ibid., pp. 35, 427.

[75] Ibid., p. 454.

[76] Gustaf Aulen, *Christus Victor*, trans. A. G. Hebert (London: SPCK, 1931), pp. 17–18.

[77] Ibid., p. 20   [78] Ibid., p. 92.

[79] Ibid., p. 83.   [80] Ibid., pp. 68–69.

[81] Ibid., Chapter Six.   [82] Ibid., pp. 72–74.

83 Ibid., pp. 82, 175.   84 Ibid., pp. 21, 72.

85 Ibid., p. 107.

86 Ibid., p. 75.   87 Ibid., pp. 151–152.

88 Ibid., p. 71. See also *The Christian Faith*, trans E. H. Wahlstrom (Philadelphia: The Muhlenberg Press, 1962), pp. 196–213.

89 John Macquarrie, *Principles of Christian Theology* (New York: Scribners, 1966), pp. 286–290.

90 F. W. Dillistone, *The Christian Understanding of Atonement*, Chapter Three.

91 See H. E. W. Turner, *The Patristic Doctrine of Redemption* (London: A. R. Mowbray and Co. Ltd., 1952), p. 121.

92 Don S. Browning, *Atonement and Psychotherapy* (Philadelphia: The Westminster Press, 1966), Preface.

93 Ibid., p. 95.   94 Ibid., p. 244.

95 Ibid., p. 115.   96 Ibid., p. 249.

97 Ibid., p. 175.   98 Ibid., p. 112.

99 Ibid., pp. 208–211.   100 Ibid., p. 241.

101 Ibid., p. 242.

4
Emergence of a New Theory

Of the eight theories of atonement surveyed in the previous chapter, one had as its setting Neoplatonism; two had legal settings; one had a moral, and one a military setting; and three, Campbell's, Rashdall's, and Browning's, were set in the realm of interpersonal relationships. I believe that interpersonal relationships constitute the most promising setting for a modern theory of atonement, but these three theories will not do because none of them successfully expresses the victorious achievement of Christ. Vicarious repentance, moral influence, and psychotherapeutic empathy do not convey the sense that Christ did something once for all that changed everything for mankind. Although models taken from interpersonal relationships appeal strongly to us, we may well doubt if they are capable of communicating the objectivity of Christ's work.

In the middle of the nineteenth century a new model of atonement emerged; taken from the realm of interpersonal relationships, it is capable of expressing Christ's objective achievement. I call it the theory of costly forgiveness. Today it is widely employed, but ironically it is rarely treated as a distinct theory, being confused instead with other theories which also have a personal setting, particularly the moral influence theory. In this chapter we will examine this theory of costly forgiveness in the theologies of Horace Bushnell,

H. R. Mackintosh, D. M. Baillie, and Leonard Hodgson.

Horace Bushnell: Forgiveness Through Self-Propitiation

Horace Bushnell was an American theologian whose writings were published after the middle of the nineteenth century. Until ill health forced him to retire, he was pastor of a Congregational church in Hartford, Connecticut. He is well known for his ideas about Christian nurture, religious language, and the Trinity. He saw himself as being in the middle of theological controversy, with New England Calvinism on his right offering a theology no one could believe and Unitarianism on his left offering a theology not worth believing.

He wrote two books about the meaning of Christ's death, *The Vicarious Sacrifice* (1866) and *Forgiveness and Law*, published posthumously (1874). The customary interpretation of Bushnell is that the two books present essentially the same theory of atonement, a moral influence view like the one Hastings Rashdall was to offer fifty years later. I feel, however, that this is incorrect, and that in *Forgiveness and Law* Bushnell offered a theory which is so different from that in *The Vicarious Sacrifice* that it should be regarded as a new one.

We can best see what was new in *Forgiveness and Law* by contrasting it with *The Vicarious Sacrifice*. We shall begin, therefore, with a summary of Bushnell's original theory of atonement as found in the earlier book. We have selected seven leading themes under which to present the summary.

1. First, Bushnell began, we must recognize that God loves all men, even though they are sinners. There can be no question of the cross purchasing God's love toward men.

2. Second, Bushnell argued, if you love someone, you will

have to suffer for him. This is an unusual point, but Bushnell was quite firm on it: "Love is a principle essentially vicarious in its own nature, identifying the subject with others, so as to suffer their adversities and pain, and taking on itself the burden of their evils." [1] A mother suffers that way for her child.[2] Vicarious sacrifice, far from being rare, is the most natural thing in the world, and it is true of God's love just as it is of human love. God suffers vicariously for those he loves. Bushnell never doubted for a moment that God is passible or capable of suffering, though there is a long tradition in Christian theology which says that God is not passible.[3]

3. We shall omit the third point for now. In *The Vicarious Sacrifice* Bushnell moved on directly to the fourth point, but in *Forgiveness and Law* he added an extra point here.

4. Fourth, Christ revealed to men this vicarious suffering of God. He did this by his own life and especially by his cross. "What then was Christ in His vicarious feeling and sacrifice, what in His Gethsemane, but a revelation in time of just that love that had been struggling always in God's bosom?" [4] By loving in this way and so revealing God's love to man, Christ accumulated a power that can come in no other way, the moral power to transform people without coercing them.[5] His resurrection proved that he had this moral power.[6]

5. Fifth, Christ used his power to transform men, to heal, regenerate, and restore the souls of men.[7] This was his purpose in coming into the world. The concept of moral transformation by revelation is the heart of Bushnell's teaching in *The Vicarious Sacrifice*. It is quite appropriate, therefore, to call this a moral influence theory.

6. Sixth, it is only by making men good that the moral law can be satisfied. Righteousness cannot be content until men

are good. This is the only concept of satisfaction appropriate to a theory of atonement.

7. Finally, Bushnell rejected the idea of Calvin that Christ accepted substitutionary punishment for men. He also rejected the idea[8] that Christ suffered penally because that was the only way that God could forgive the world yet still make it clear that he does not take sin lightly. He also rejected the view of Anselm that Christ somehow provided satisfaction for man's sins.

Now let us compare this theory point by point with that in Bushnell's later book, Forgiveness and Law.

1. First, Bushnell continued to affirm that God loves men. This is still the presupposition of his theology.

2. Second, he continued to believe that love involves making a vicarious sacrifice for the one you love and that this is true of God just as it is of man. He believed that God is passible.

3. Third—and this is the new point—Bushnell came to the conclusion that this vicarious suffering of God is far more than a matter of sympathy with fallen men. God suffers in order to master certain feelings which might have led him to reject men even though he loved them. Bushnell called this function of God's suffering self-propitiation. "Nothing will ever accomplish the real and true forgiveness, but to make cost in the redeemer, such cost as new tempers and liquifies the reluctant nature. And this cost will be his propitiation of himself." [9]

Once again Bushnell argued from human experience. We usually assume that men can forgive others without any propitiation, but this is not true.[10]

A good man lives in the unquestionable sway of universal love to his kind. If then one of them does him a bitter wrong, will he therefore launch an absolute forgiveness on him? If he were nothing but love—if he were no complete moral nature—he might. But he is a complete moral nature, having other involuntary sentiments that come into play along-side of love, and partly for its sake—the sense of being rent by wrong, indignation against wrong done to others, disgust to what is loathsome, comtempt of lies, hatred of oppression, anger hot against cruel inhumanities—all these animosities, or revulsions of feeling, fasten their grip on the malefactor's sins and refuse to let go.[11]

If a man is to forgive, therefore, he must somehow deal with these feelings. He cannot deny them, for they are good—a good man ought to hate evil. Yet unless he deals with them, he will be unable to forgive. "They require to be somehow mastered, and somehow to remain." [12] This can be done in one way only, by that vicarious suffering which is love. Such suffering propitiates these feelings, and this prepares the way for forgiveness. "Two things are necessary; first, such a sympathy with the wrong doing party as virtually takes his nature; and secondly, a making cost in that nature by suffering, or expense, or painstaking sacrifice and labor." [13] "And when it is done thoroughly enough to configure and new-tone the forgiving party as well as the forgiven, he in so far becomes himself a reconciled or propitated man, as truly as the other has become a forgiven or restored man." [14]

This is the new element in Bushnell's theology: that forgiveness cannot be easy but must be prepared for in a costly way. "So far from its being an absurd thing to speak of a propitiation as the necessary precondition of forgiveness, no human creature will ever keep himself reconciled to his kind, without finding how in some of its degrees to practice it. Instead of being a great theologic mystery, it is even the common exigent of life." [15]

This is true of God as well as of man. God suffers vicariously to propitiate himself so as to be prepared to forgive men their sins.

Bushnell himself did not use the word *objective* to describe his theory of atonement. But the new element in his view is objective in the sense that forgiveness has been achieved at the specific cost of God's sufferings. In *The Vicarious Sacrifice* Bushnell had spoken only of man being reconciled to God. In *Forgiveness and Law* he spoke as well of God being reconciled to man.[16] In *The Vicarious Sacrifice* he had felt that the word *propitiation* was to be employed only as an accommodation: Men feel that God has been propitiated, though of course in fact no such thing has occurred or is necessary. But in *Forgiveness and Law* propitiation has become a great and costly reality in the life of God. [17]

It is so objective that Bushnell can speak of forgiveness as something which the offended person does without any reference at all to the response of the offender: "The forgiveness is in you potentially complete, even though it should never be actually sealed upon the offender. You have taken his sin upon you in the cost you have borne for his sake." [18]

4. Bushnell's fourth point is similar to his fourth point in *The Vicarious Sacrifice*. Christ has revealed this self-propitiating vicarious sacrifice. In fact, he may even be said to have participated in it. "Christ is not other than God in any such way that his propitiation is any the less truly a self-propitiation of God." [19] Christ did not, however, make the entire divine sacrifice himself. "The transactional matter of Christ's life and death is a specimen chapter, so to speak, of the infinite book that records the eternal going on of God's blessed nature within." [20] Since God has always suffered to prepare to forgive men, he has always been ready to forgive.

Nevertheless it is Christ who, by revealing this of God, accumulates the moral power to transform men.

5. Fifth, this revelation of God does in fact transform men. Bushnell was as concerned as ever to assert the moral influence of Christ's life and death.[21]

6. Sixth, it is still this transformation of men which satisfies the demands of the moral law.

7. Seventh, Bushnell rejected as firmly as ever the penal view of Christ's death and the idea that Christ in any sense provided a compensation for men's sins.

Most interpreters of Bushnell have regarded his view as a moral influence theory. This is true of his earlier book, but in Forgiveness and Law he introduced a new theory, the theory of costly forgiveness. The meaning of the death of Christ is more than that God loves or even that he suffers; it is that he suffers in order to provide forgiveness for men.

How can we tell that this is new in Bushnell's theology? One important indication is that whereas forgiveness dominates the second book, it scarcely appears in the first.[22] He is dealing with a new subject. In The Vicarious Sacrifice he had taken forgiveness for granted, just as Rashdall was to do half a century later. But in Forgiveness and Law, so far from taking forgiveness for granted, Bushnell's chief concern was to show that the costly prerequisite for forgiveness, divine suffering, had been revealed in Christ.

This fact encourages us to take seriously Bushnell's own testimony that he was proposing a new theory. "It will be understood, I presume, that I suppose the two revised statements, or solutions of doctrine I am now going to propound, to be really new. I frankly allow that I do, and also am frankly confessing that in this simple fact my courage and confidence are most weakened by misgivings." [23]

We shall take Bushnell at his word. He has offered us a

new way of seeing the meaning of the cross, as a revelation of and a part of a self-propitiation which God made as a vicarious sacrifice in order to be prepared to forgive men of their sins. Bushnell retained the moral influence view, but added to it an objective and costly work of forgiveness. H. Sheldon Smith has commented that throughout his life Bushnell attempted to go beyond a purely subjective theory: "The question that baffled him most was how to give Christ's work a truly objective character." [24] It is my judgment that he succeeded in doing this in Forgiveness and Law.

Now I shall attempt to provide an evaluation of Bushnell's new theory.

1. Bushnell dropped the models and legal settings which he inherited from New England Calvinism. He replaced them with a model taken from the world of interpersonal relationships, the model of forgiveness. This is his most important contribution, for it is this model in this setting that provides us today with our best understanding of the meaning of Christ's death.[25]

2. Bushnell recognized that forgiveness, unlike indulgence, is costly. It is in the costliness of forgiveness that we are to locate the objective meaning of the death of Christ. Bushnell has here hit upon the most important clue of our understanding of Christ's death. So far as I have been able to discover, he was the first to do so.

3. He saw God as eternally suffering in order to provide forgiveness. Thus Christ's work was part of God's self-propitiation, and also a revelation of it, but it was not in itself the ground of all forgiveness. On this point Bushnell was mistaken, as I shall try to show below.

4. Since he did not see Christ's sacrifice as the cost of divine forgiveness, it was not necessary for Bushnell to analyze precisely in what sense Christ suffered. For exam-

ple, were Christ's sufferings made important because they
were a consequence of his obedience? Was it important that
they were a direct consequence of man's sin? These are
questions which the theory of costly forgiveness ought to
answer so that the relationship between cost and forgiveness
will be transparently clear.

5. Bushnell felt that God was obligated to love men in this
costly way. He was not obligated to men, but to his own
righteousness, to make cost so as to forgive.[26] I believe that
Bushnell was mistaken about this. What God did in Christ he
did in his freedom, not by obligation.

6. It is an inexplicable and odd fact that Bushnell did not
attempt to show a connection between the two subjects
which most concerned him, namely, forgiveness and the
transformation of a man's character. This connection is essential to the theology of costly forgiveness.

7. Seventh, as we have seen, Bushnell's great achievement was to understand Christ's sufferings in the context of
interpersonal relations. He failed to see, however, that God's
punishment of sin could also be set in the interpersonal
context. In both his books, Bushnell left punishment in its
legal context. "Forgiveness, we thus find, puts a man personally right with God, but it does not put him right with
law, and it is not easy to see that anything can." [27] But if
forgiveness is to be understood in personal terms, so must
punishment, because the withholding of punishment is a part
of forgiveness. The theory of costly forgiveness must integrate
its view of forgiveness and punishment into the setting of
interpersonal relations, or it cannot stand as a unified theory.

8. Finally, Bushnell felt obligated to reject the legal and
transactional view of the past. I believe, however, that it is
possible to appreciate them if we evaluate them within their
own settings. Bushnell might have appraised Anselm's view
on its own terms, as a view arising out of the feudal world

and the penitential system. Instead he measured it by the moral standards which apply in the realm of interpersonal relationships within which his own moral influence view and later his costly forgiveness view were set. Naturally when it was measured this way, Anselm's view failed. For example, Bushnell rejected the idea that Christ provided an extra virtue (supererogation) to offer to God on man's behalf. It is true that there is no room for supererogation in the setting of interpersonal relationships. But there was room for it in the penitential setting which Anselm used. When each of these two models is evaluated by standards appropriate to itself it succeeds in explaining the meaning of Christ's sacrifice. Ironically, Anselm was saying identically the same thing that Bushnell was but in his own way. One clear indication of this is that, having rejected the idea of transaction over and over, Bushnell unwittingly used the word "transactional" to describe his own view! [28]

It has been necessary to examine and appraise Bushnell's views closely because he was the first to employ the model of costly forgiveness to explain the meaning of Christ's death. Several writers since Bushnell have used the same model, and we shall now observe some of them, though in less detail. Our chief concern in looking at them is to see where they differed from Bushnell and to determine whether or not their innovations were improvements on his basic theory.

H. R. Mackintosh: Forgiveness as Christianity's Message

H. R. Mackintosh was a shrewd Scottish theologian who has had an important influence on theology in Britain and elsewhere. He was at the height of his power when he wrote *The Christian Experience of Forgiveness* in 1927, and he always regarded it as his most important book.

His understanding of forgiveness was that it is always a result of costly suffering, and he acknowledged that it is to Bushnell that we owe this insight.[29] "When by self-conquest which even bystanders may see to be noble the injured man (or, as it may be, woman), refusing to ignore moral realities, yet reaching over and beyond the wrong to knit up the old ties of communion, attains to the act of deep pure pardon, the act presupposes and is predicted by costly suffering." [30] So the sacrifice of Christ is "the cost of forgiveness to God." [31]

Mackintosh argued that it is the costliness of forgiveness that sets it apart from indulgence: "It is no poor or cheap forgiveness He imparts, but one flowing from unmeasured expenditure of Spirit and will." [32] He contrasted his view with the moral influence theory. It is not enough to say God can forgive by fiat and that Christ merely revealed God's forgiveness and encouraged men to accept it; for then forgiveness would have been more like indulgence.[33] Mackintosh felt that the cross provides the only assurance that God really loves men.[34] Bushnell, who began with the assumption that God loves men, would have found this hard to understand.

Mackintosh emphasized more than Bushnell that what God does by his suffering is to overcome his own moral objection to being reconciled to sinners. Where Bushnell had spoken vaguely of God "liquifying" his feelings of hostility so as to accept sinners because of his holiness, Mackintosh quite definitely spoke of God having hindrances to accepting sinners because of his holiness. "What holy love in God required as a condition of pardon, more correctly as a living element in pardon, was . . . such a sacrificial manifestation of his own nature as must, if God and man be of one moral order, form the only conceivable medium of forgiveness." [35]

Mackintosh felt that the incarnation of Jesus was more essential to this work of God than Bushnell did. "The atonement has neither substance nor efficacy apart from the assurance that in Jesus God is personally present." [36] In fact, "The sacrifice of Christ *is* the sacrifice of God, in which He makes our burden His own and puts away sin by the surrender of Himself." [37] Christ therefore did more than reveal God's forgiving love, he conveyed it to men. [38]

But Mackintosh did not feel that Jesus' sufferings by themselves constituted the price God paid to forgive men. They were rather an index to God's eternal suffering: "The electric current that pervades the whole wire flashes into light at its sensitive point; so the timeless pain of God over human evil becomes visible in Christ's passion." [39]

To this point, Mackintosh has more or less elaborated Bushnell's model. But he also added four important new ideas, three of them true and one, in my judgment, a mistake.

1. Where Bushnell had treated forgiveness as if it were an important part of Christianity, Mackintosh treated it as if it were the very essence of Christianity. This is what Christian faith means: God forgives sinners in this costly way. A Christian is one who confesses: "I believe in God who forgives sin through Jesus Christ." [40]

Mackintosh felt that this fact is evident in the New Testament. The life of Jesus was characterized by a costly seeking out and accepting of society's worst sinners.[41] His proclamation of the kingdom of God was a message that God receives sinners.[42] Jesus insisted that he had the right to forgive sins. Forgiveness was present in Jesus in a unique way, and human experience testifies to his power to forgive: "It is a simple psychological fact, I am persuaded, that the only people in the world today who live in the glad consciousness that their sins have been forgiven are those who have encountered Jesus." [43]

Forgiveness was also the message of Paul, who knew it under the name of *justification*. Of forgiveness and justification Mackintosh wrote: "How these ideas, if rightly interpreted, really differ, is hard to see." [44] Mackintosh argued the identity of forgiveness and justification throughout chapter 5 of his book. In this, his book is very unlike Bushnell's. Bushnell resisted the traditional view of justification because of its legal setting. Mackintosh shrewdly recognized that Paul was expressing in legal terms the same thing that Jesus had expressed by his life and message as forgiveness. That is the Christian message, that God forgives sinners at great cost to himself.

2. The second new concept which Mackintosh introduced was that there is a direct connection between a man's being forgiven by God and his being transformed into a good man. Bushnell regrettably had ignored this connection. In a chapter entitled "The Moral Inspiration of Forgiveness," Mackintosh argued that forgiveness "by its nature implies the breaking of sin's power." [45] The very concept of forgiveness has a liberating effect. A man's new fellowship with God, his awareness of God's presence with him in the moral struggle, and his new insight into God's character of forgiving love, all influence a man for good.[46] A forgiven man has been delivered from his self-centeredness, and this assists his moral development.[47]

Mackintosh has shown how transformation actually comes about. God is not merely a judge watching to see if men measure up. Nor does he displace human freedom and efforts and coerce men into goodness. Rather, at great cost to himself he forgives them of their sins, and this forgiveness is the beginning of a relationship in which God exercises the most powerful moral influence possible in the life of a free man.

It is sometimes argued that if God completely and freely forgives a man of all his sins, the man will have no motivation for becoming a better person. Mackintosh saw clearly that the opposite is true. A man remains trapped in a vicious cycle of self-justification and self-pity until God completely forgives him and takes him out of himself; only then is he freed to become a better person.[48]

3. Both of Bushnell's books were about God's vicarious sacrifice for individuals. To Mackintosh's great credit, he carried these ideas about forgiveness over into the life of the church. He argued that the church is made up of people who, having experienced forgiveness themselves, proclaim the message of God's forgiveness to the world and then live a life together that validates that message. "It is only when the air is warm with brotherhood that the Gospel sounds true." [49] So the church has an indispensable role in taking God's forgiveness to the world: "Were the Church to disappear, the reality of Divine pardon would disappear along with it." [50] Forgiveness is the hardest of all moral tasks, but it is precisely forgiveness, costly forgiveness, which God requires of his forgiven people.[51]

4. The fourth new idea which Mackintosh introduced was, in my judgment, a mistake. He said that Jesus at his death was not only suffering in order to forgive sinners but he was also bearing the punishment of men's sins. "For us, with us, He there bowed under the Father's judgment on sin, confessing the sinfulness of wrong and its utter evil in God's sight." [52]

Earlier in the book, Mackintosh had attempted to argue that punishment is a personal more than a legal idea.[53] The worst punishment of all, he said, is to be isolated from God.[54] But in chapter 9 he seemed to have forgotten that, and he insisted that Christ's death was God's legal judgment upon sin, a judgment which Christ accepted on man's behalf.[55]

This seems to be an attempt to hold together two different models for Christ's work, the personal model of forgiveness and the legal model of acquittal and punishment. I do not think it succeeds; it cannot be consistently held. Would Mackintosh have actually said that God isolated Christ from himself? I doubt it. Bushnell had kept the personal and legal models separate in his books. Mackintosh tried to put them together and failed. Are we then to conclude that it is not possible to state the relationship between forgiveness and punishment? So long as punishment is thought of in legal terms, it is impossible. But if punishment is conceived strictly in personal terms, then its relationship to forgiveness becomes clear.

D. M. Baillie: Forgiveness as an Objective Achievement

It was another Scottish theologian, D. M. Baillie, who presented the theology of atonement as costly forgiveness in what is in my judgment its finest brief statement. His book, *God Was in Christ*, published in 1948, was concerned principally with Christology, but the final chapters were about the meaning of Christ's death. In them he argued, first, that men today may deny their sin and their need of forgiveness, but they need it nevertheless and need it desperately.

Having established that, he asked, Why atonement? Cannot God simply forgive? His answer was clear: Forgiveness without cost is not true forgiveness at all but good-natured indulgence, and God is not indulgent. "Does the whole process of reconciliation cost Him nothing? Is His forgiveness facile and cheap?" [56] Baillie compared God's costly forgiveness with that of a friend who forgives one who betrays him.

But man's betrayal of God is infinitely worse, and the cost of forgiving it is "an 'atonement' which is the most difficult, the most supernatural, the costliest thing in the world." [57]

Baillie's indebtedness to Bushnell and Mackintosh was very great. To their insights he added four of his own, all of great value.

1. He was more successful than Bushnell and Mackintosh at keeping his language about the cross strictly within the context of interpersonal relationships. "In theological argument on this subject we are apt to forget that we are dealing with a realm of personal relationships and nothing else." [58] But Baillie did not forget.

It is in dealing with punishment that a writer is most likely to fall back into the legal setting. Baillie insisted, to his great credit, that punishment also is personal relationship: it is man's alienation from God.[59] It is the obverse side of God's love. It is not at all legal, nor is it an impersonal principle working itself out in men's lives. [60] It is a personal response to a sinner, and when a sinner is forgiven, the divine personal punishment ceases and is replaced with the divine personal forgiveness.[61] Baillie succeeded in keeping all of his explanation of the cross in personal terms.

2. Baillie also provided the most explicit discussion to date of the relation between the historical suffering of Christ and the eternal divine suffering. In a section entitled "Historical and Eternal Atonement" he wrote, "It is not that the historical episode is a mere symbol of something 'timeless': it is actually a part (the incarnate part) of the eternal divine sin-bearing." [62] He was quite explicit that God himself experiences suffering because of man's sin: "It all takes place within the life of God Himself." [63] Christ's suffering in time is "that outcropping of divine atonement in human history which makes His mercy effectual for our salvation." [64] Al-

though the atonement is eternal, Christ's work is in a real
sense finished and perfect.[65]

Baillie did not explain how Christ's work can be both an
outcropping of an eternal work and also finished. He regarded it as a paradox, a consequence of man's inability to
state more specifically what is finished about Christ's work
by giving attention to what it is that Christ suffered.[66]

3. Baillie was the first theologian, so far as I can tell, to
insist that the costly suffering which precedes divine forgiveness is an objective achievement of God. In a section
entitled "Objective and Subjective Atonement" he wrote: "It
is only out of the suffering of such inexorable love that the
true forgiveness, as distinct from an indulgent amnesty,
could ever come. That is the objective process of atonement
that goes on in the very life of God." [67] It is now more than
thirty years since Baillie's book was published, yet, so far as I
have been able to discover, Baillie's suggestion has been
largely ignored. Thus it is still argued that Bushnell, for
example, had a moral influence or subjective view of atonement, whereas it is in fact exactly the view which Baillie
called "objective."

4. Finally, Baillie tied this understanding of forgiveness
more closely to the entire biblical message than any previous
writer had done. His argument was that the main ideas of the
Bible developed in a certain sequence. First, Israel had a
sacrificial system, but it was of value only for ceremonial
offenses and had no provision for moral sins. Second, the
prophets insisted that it is moral sins that matter and also
that God will forgive anyone who repents. Third, after the
exile, sacrifices were provided for moral sins. Finally, the
New Testament tied together in a unique way the prophetic
insistence that God freely forgives those who repent with the
priestly insistence that forgiveness comes only by sacrifice,

simply by affirming that in Christ God himself bears the cost of forgiveness.[68] Christ's entire life and ministry were characterized by his acceptance of unworthy people, so it is accurate to say that historically as well as theologically he died for sinners, in that it was his conscious attitude toward sinners that led to his rejection by the nation's leaders.[69]

We may summarize Baillie's contributions to the new theory thus: (1) He consistently kept his model for atonement in the context of personal relationships, even when dealing with punishment. (2) He specifically raised the question of the relation between Christ's historical suffering and God's eternal suffering (although I happen not to accept his conclusion). (3) He argued quite properly that the suffering which forgiveness entails is an objective and not just a subjective atonement. (4) He integrated the idea of costly forgiveness into the entire, biblical message better than had been done heretofore.

Leonard Hodgson: Forgiveness as an Historical Event

Leonard Hodgson, an English theologian who died in 1969, published in 1951 a series of lectures entitled *The Doctrine of the Atonement.* Hodgson held a very definite view about how God has revealed himself to man. He said that God's revelation is given in deeds rather than words.[70] This left him free to say that the words with which the New Testament writers described the meaning of Christ's death were simply those that lay at their disposal. "It was natural that their expositions of the doctrine of the atonement should be set in the thought forms and expressed in the language of Jewish sacrificial worship." [71] Theologians today, who do not participate in animal sacrifices and for whom therefore those sacrificial images are not natural, are free to seek the models which best capture the meaning of the cross for themselves.[72] The model which Hodgson himself used is the one we are calling costly forgiveness.

1. Hodgson thought of forgiveness, first of all, as "an activity in which the injured man can engage irrespective of the continuing attitude of his injuror." [73] Even before the sinner repents, the injured man can be enduring the pain which the sin has caused, in such a way as to absorb its power to produce further evil.[74] Later on, when the sinner repents, he will find forgiveness ready and waiting.

2. Hodgson argued that the suffering which provides forgiveness is suffering which is caused specifically by the sins to be forgiven. It is also suffering accepted in such a way as to "give place to goodwill and love." [75] This kind of suffering is difficult and costly, but it is indispensable for forgiveness, for "the essence of forgiveness is the taking of pain due to sin in such a way as to absorb and cut short its power to produce further evil, to treat it as raw material for increasing the world's output of goodness." [76] In effect what Hodgson was doing at this point was incorporating the idea of Christ's death as a victory into the model of costly forgiveness by insisting that the effects of Christ's forgiveness are characterized by victorious triumph.

3. Forgiveness in this sense is the only way in which the power of sin can be neutralized. The reason is that a sinner can never be really liberated from his guilt until he is sure that his sin will not go on destroying things indefinitely.[77] The Christian gospel is the good news that God himself has in Christ so absorbed the evil effects of sin that their power has been broken, cut short.

4. This brings us to Hodgson's major contribution to the doctrine of the atonement, namely, his affirmation of the finality of Christ's work in history. Hodgson sometimes said

that "Jesus reveals the divine forgiveness," [78] but the real
emphasis of his book is upon "something accomplished,
something done" in the events of Jesus' history.[79] He speaks
of "an absoluteness, a qualitative perfection" in Jesus' sacrifice.[80] "Once for all, in the history of this world, God, who
is both the source and the object of all the acts of His crea-
tures, has won the right to forgive their sins without the least
diminution of His eternal goodness which is the ground of
all our hope." [81]

For Bushnell, Mackintosh, and Baillie, Christ's sufferings
were a revelation of the divine suffering which is forgiveness, and also a part of the divine suffering which forgives.
For Hodgson, however, Christ's historical suffering was itself the divine suffering which provides the divine forgiveness. "We need to be able to believe," he wrote, "that because of what God has done in Christ forgiveness is ready for
every sinner that repents." [82] Thus Hodgson felt that Christ's
work was final in a way the earlier writers did not, and
therefore was objective in a way they had not realized. This is,
in my judgment, a very important step, and it more than
fulfills Hodgson's hope that he would "make some contribution" to the doctrine of atonement." [83]

What was there in Hodgson's theology that did not appear
in the theologies of Bushnell, Mackintosh, and Baillie, that
suggested to him the idea that God in Christ "once for all"
suffered to forgive all sins? There were, I think, two things.
First, each of the earlier three writers jettisoned or radically
reinterpreted the traditional doctrine that God is impassible.
They felt that since God is personal he can suffer, and it was
natural for them to argue that he suffers eternally because of
man's sins.

Hodgson, however, retained the doctrine that God cannot
suffer.[84] He said that God-in-himself "must be thought of as

impassible." [85] However, God has voluntarily created a
world of men to whom he is related in both active and
passive ways. Thus God voluntarily accepts passivity or
passibility. Apparently Hodgson felt (he is a little unclear on
this point) that it was only in Christ that God accepted the
passive role which we know of as suffering. Because
Hodgson felt that God-in-himself is not passible, he naturally understood the historical suffering of Jesus as God's
once-for-all suffering to forgive.

The second strand of Hodgson's theology which contributed to the accent of finality which he put upon the atonement concerned the incarnation. The three earlier theologians of costly forgiveness accepted the idea that Christ was
fully God as well as fully man; indeed, and for Mackintosh
especially, the idea of costly forgiveness could hardly exist
apart from the incarnation.

Nevertheless, Hodgson had a distinctive way of presenting
the doctrine of the incarnation. After affirming unequivoc-
ally that Jesus is divine ("It is essential to the Christian faith
to believe that Jesus of Nazareth was incarnate God" [86]), he
asked what it is to be a man. He said that to be a man is to be
the subject of experiences mediated through a body in space
and time. Therefore, we today express the orthodox teaching
about Christ "by speaking of the incarnation as the entry by
the eternal Second Person of the Trinity upon the experience
of life as a man upon earth. The life was genuinely a human
life, a human in mind as well as in body. But He who was
living that life was God." [87] God, when he was thus incarnate, accepted all kinds of human experiences, including the
experience of suffering the consequences of sins. Therefore
it was then, in the history of the world, that God suffered to
forgive sins, once for all. Hodgson's strong, clear, contemporary view of the incarnation led him to affirm the historical

achievement of forgiveness in the sufferings of Christ.

So far we have dealt with Hodgson's contributions to the theology of costly forgiveness. Now we must look at three other subjects in his writing about which, in my judgment, there are serious questions: punishment, the necessity of the cross, and the cosmic aspects of Christ's work.

1. Hodgson held a very definite view of punishment. First, it cannot take place between individuals. *"It is an activity which by its very nature can only exist between a community and a member of itself."* [88] He italicized these words because it was an important point to him.

Second, the essence of punishment is isolation or dissociation. "Punishment is essentially this disowning by a community of acts done by its members." [89]

Third, this dissociation of the members is painful for the offender. "The expression of the fact (of disapproval), if it is to be effective, must inevitably be painful. Hence the inseparable connection between the idea of punishment and pain." [90]

Fourth, punishment is retributive. That is, it is done in response to a sin. "It is the retrospective aspect that makes the action punishment." [91]

Fifth, punishment may be done "in such a way as to reform and to deter." [92] Since God loves men and wishes not only to respond to men's sin but also to respond to it in such a way as to help the man become better, his punishment is always reformatory as well as retributive.

Sixth, the world is distorted by evil. One unfortunate consequence of this is that it is not always the guilty who suffer for their sin; often the innocent suffer the consequences of the sins of the guilty.[93]

So far, Hodgson's view of punishment seems to me to be true with a minor exception: I do not find it necessary to

restrict punishment to communities, for I feel that an individual has the right, and in fact the responsibility, to dissociate himself from an evildoer and to disown his acts.
Except for that, Hodgson's view seems to me to be correct.

But Hodgson went on to raise the question about Jesus'
death, and he said that Jesus accepted divine punishment.
Vicarious punishment, he argued, was brought into disre-
pute by those who separated Christ from God or at least the
human nature of Christ from its divine nature. But the sep-
aration is false; Christ was true God and true man, so
"Punisher and Punished are one." [94] Christ accepted as the
Father's will for him the law that sin produces pain. God
himself accepted his own punishment for man's sin. "He
wills that sin shall be punished, but He does not will that sin
shall be punished without also willing that the punishment
shall fall on Himself." [95] This, argued Hodgson, is the essence
of divine forgiveness: the acceptance of the precise pain
which he, the righteous Judge, had determined was the appropriate fate of the sinner. "Now we may go a step further,
and see in the suffering of Christ not only His endorsement of
God's wrath against sin, but also the revelation of the manner
of God's forgiveness." [96] Even more definitely Hodgson
wrote: "He embraces that self-punishment which combines
the activities of punishing and forgiving." [97]

In much of this Hodgson was mistaken. The source of his
confusion lay in the ambiguity of the idea that Jesus suffered
the consequences of sin. We shall devote chapter 6 to an
analysis of this concept. Right now the important thing is to
notice that though Jesus did experience some of the consequences of sin, it is by no means clear that he experienced
them all. Within the parameters which Hodgson himself
established it is inaccurate to say that what Jesus experienced was punishment. Did Jesus experience a divine dis-

sociation and disowning of his action? Was divine retribution directed to him, or an effort made by God to reform him? It is true that the pain Jesus suffered is the sort of thing which, if experienced by a sinner, we might think of in terms of God's punishment, but that is a very different matter from saying that in Christ God willed that punishment should fall on himself.

2. My second criticism of Hodgson is that he attempted to demonstrate that the death of Christ was a necessity to God. His argument began by asking what options were open to a person who had been sinned against. He thought there were only three. First, he could ignore the sin. Bushnell, Mackintosh, and Baillie had called this indulgence and urged us not to confuse it with forgiveness. Hodgson's view was even stronger. To ignore sin, he argued, is connivance. To ignore sin is to become implicated in it. The only way to avoid this is to dissociate oneself from the sinful act, that is, to punish.[98]

Punishment is the second option open to one who has been sinned against. But punishment alone does not rescue the sinner. Even more important, when we punish a wrongdoer, we are tempted to become embittered and vengeful, which is to allow the evil effects of the sin to continue. It is very difficult, perhaps impossible, to avoid the temptation to bitterness (Hodgson was a little unclear about this). Clearly, punishment alone will not do. Hodgson said this about a community: "The maintenance of its good life is threatened in two ways: as the source of the (sinful) act the misuse of its life and power solicits its connivance at evil; as the object of the (sinful) act its suffering tempts it to embittered vengeance. It must punish if it is to overcome the former temptation. It must forgive if it is to resist the latter. How can it do both?" [99]

The only solution left open, according to Hodgson, is the kind of forgiveness which accepts the painful consequences of sins, including, as we have seen, the consequences we ordinarily associate with punishment.

Hodgson's argument was that if God is not to connive at sins, he must punish them; if he punishes them he will be tempted to become embittered; to avoid this he must forgive them; and the only way he can forgive them is to suffer their consequences, including their penal ones.

This, it seems to me, is not correct. It is the most persuasive answer I know of to the question, Why did God become man? But it does not work. The argument is mistaken at several points. It is not correct to say that the only way to avoid embittered vengeance is to accept the punishment of sins oneself. As a matter of fact, it is possible to punish a sinner without being tempted to bitterness. For that matter, if you accept the painful consequences of another's sin, that could in itself tempt you to further bitterness. Hodgson failed to show why the death of Christ was necessary for God. In the next chapter we shall present an alternative to this view.

3. Finally, Hodgson made a robust presentation of the cosmic dimensions of Christ's work. He set it in as large a context as possible, that of evolution. "This created universe, this evolutionary process, has not developed and is not developing straightforwardly towards the fulfillment of the divine purpose." [100] The world is marked by evil in four forms: ignorance, ugliness, suffering, and sin. [101] God is concerned to rid his universe of all four forms of evil. "Human wickedness, the latest to appear, is the worst evil and the hard core of the problem of evil." [102] This is because it takes place in men who are the climax of God's creative activity. "We see what has been called the cosmic signifi-

cance of the atonement when we think of God waiting until the power of evil has reached its peak in the corruption of human goodness and then intervening to initiate the process of rescuing His creation from its grip." [103] By freeing man from sin by means of costly forgiveness, God initiated a process whose final result will be the rescue of the universe from all the four forms of evil. "Sinners converted, cleansed and forgiven are commissioned and empowered, through the arts and sciences and in every department of life, to bring all the natural world to the obedience of Christ." [104]

Hodgson's vision is breathtaking, but is it true? Two things about it worry me. First, is God really concerned about ugliness and ignorance in quite the way Hodgson says? Are they evil in just the same sense that suffering and sin are? If they are, and if God is concerned about them in this way, it would be helpful if this were demonstrated more fully than Hodgson has done.[105]

Second, there is a vital link missing in Hodgson's movement from a forgiven sinner to a transformed universe. This missing link is the middle one, namely, a transformed sinner, a man who finds the forgiveness of his sins the first step in a new life in which his freedom is respected and his character nevertheless changed for the better. To express it in the traditional language of theology, Hodgson has not provided us with the connection between justification and sanctification.

Except for this, however, his cosmic vision is a very helpful one. To put it simply, Christians believe that there is an important sense in which Christ by his sacrifice provided man with all that is necessary for a whole, full life for himself and for his world. Hodgson's theology is an initial step toward that goal. Others need to be taken.

The most important contribution of Leonard Hodgson was

his vision of the finality of Christ's work. That, however, has been a neglected theme since Hodgson gave his lectures, so far as I am able to tell.[106] We shall take it up in the following chapter.

We began the present study by arguing that a doctrine of atonement is a theological explanation of the meaning of Christ's death which attempts to show how his sacrifice is related to a Christian's experience of being forgiven. In chapter 1 we examined three New Testament witnesses to the meaning of the cross in the contexts of eschatology, law, and ritual. In chapter 2 we sketched out the ingredients of a theory of atonement as being a model in a setting along with its history, presuppositions, capabilities and limitations, and we argued that models, though related to one time and culture, nevertheless either express or fail to express the truth about Christ's death. In chapter 3 we examined eight of the models which have been used for Christ's death at various times in church history, and we said that each one failed to satisfy us for one reason or another. Something else is wanted: a model from the setting of interpersonal relations capable of expressing the victorious achievement of Christ.

In the present chapter we have argued that during the past century a new model has been emerging, that of costly forgiveness. Although in the past it has been confused with other models, especially moral influence, it is in fact a distinct model. It has been developed in various ways by men from Bushnell to the present. I believe that it is the most promising model for understanding Christ's death that we have today. Nevertheless, as my evaluation of the theologies of Bushnell and his successors implies, it is my judgment that no theology of costly forgiveness has yet managed to use the model to its capacity. For the remainder of this book our concern will be to employ the human experience of costly forgiveness to explain as much as it is capable of explaining about the meaning of Christ's death.

NOTES

[1] Horace Bushnell, *The Vicarious Sacrifice: Grounded in Principles of Universal Obligation* (London: Alexander Strahan, 1866), p. 7.

[2] p. 11.

[3] Proponents of the theory of costly forgiveness all agree that divine suffering achieves something worthwhile, namely, forgiveness. To fail to affirm that would be to make suffering an end in itself, which is a very different matter. Perhaps a suffering man could find some comfort in the thought that God also suffers. That seems to have been the view of the Japanese theologian Kozah Kitamori. Immediately after the Second World War he wrote: "I am dissolved in the pain of God and become one with him in pain." (*Theology of the Pain of God*, p. 71.). This view seems to me to be pathological because God accepts pain for its own sake rather than as a way of receiving men. It did not occur in either of Bushnell's books.

[4] p. 32.   [5] p. 140.

[6] p. 133.   [7] p. 92.

[8] Bushnell knew this theory as the Edwardian theory, named after Jonathan Edwards. It was fully developed by Edwards' son. It first occurred in the theology of a Dutch jurist, Hugo Grotius, and is variously known as the governmental view or the rectoral view. There are traces of it in the theology of P. T. Forsyth.

[9] Horace Bushnell, *Forgiveness and Law: Grounded in Principles Interpreted by Human Analogies* (London: Hodder and Stoughton, 1874).

[10] pp. 35–36.   [11] p. 38.

[12] p. 38.   [13] p. 40.

[14] p. 41.   [15] p. 49.

[16] p. 33.   [17] p. 35.

[18] p. 44.   [19] pp. 58–59.

[20] p. 60.   [21] pp. 12–13.

[22] He mentions it on p. 91 of *The Vicarious Sacrifice* to say that it is secondary if at all true to say that Christ prepared a "possibility of forgiveness," and on pp. 300–301 to say that the New Testament never speaks of any "ground" of forgiveness. As we have seen he reverses this opinion in the second book. Of course, there may have been other references I missed.

[23] *Forgiveness and Law*, p. 14.

[24] H. Sheldon Smith, ed., *Horace Bushnell* (New York: Oxford University Press, 1965), p. 310.

[25] As we saw earlier, Campbell replaced the legal with the personal setting several years earlier than Bushnell, though not in order to employ the model of costly forgiveness.

[26] *Forgiveness and Law*, p. 62.

[27] *Forgiveness and Law*, p. 93.

[28] *Forgiveness and Law*, p. 60, quoted above p. 91.

[29] H. R. Mackintosh, *The Christian Experience of Forgiveness* (London: Nisbet and Co., Ltd., 1927), p. 185.

[30] p. 188.   [31] p. 192.

[32] p. 186.   [33] pp. 215–216.

[34] p. 217.   [35] p. 190. See also p. 28.

[36] p. 208.   [37] p. 209.

[38] p. 212.   [39] p. 216.

[40] p. 1. See also p. 17.   [41] pp. 88–95.

[42] p. 85.   [43] p. 82.

[44] p. 3.   [45] p. 252.

[46] pp. 254–255.   [47] p. 257.

[48] The connection between forgiveness and moral change had been argued for by Douglas White in a little-known book published in 1913 entitled *Forgiveness and Suffering* (p. 114). White, who was professionally a physician rather than a theologian, was apparently the first person to argue that costly forgiveness was a new theory of atonement (Preface). He also succeeded in presenting punishment in completely personal terms, with no legal overtones (p. 49), which the theory of forgiveness requires.

[49] p. 280.   [50] p. 271.

[51] p. 228.   [52] p. 222. See also pp. 205–206.

[53] Chapter Seven.   [54] p. 168.

[55] p. 198.

[56] D. M. Baillie, *God Was in Christ* (New York: Charles Scribner's Sons, 1948), p. 172.

[57] p. 174.   [58] p. 198.

[59] p. 168.   [60] p. 189.

[61] pp. 167–168.   [62] pp. 191–192.

[63] p. 188.   [64] p. 201.

[65] p. 195.   [66] p. 190.

[67] p. 198.   [68] pp. 175–177.

[69] pp. 181–184.

[70] Leonard Hodgson, *The Doctrine of the Atonement* (London: Nisbet and Co., Ltd., 1951), p. 14.

[71] p. 140.   [72] p. 141.

[73] p. 62.   [74] p. 63.

[75] p. 63.

[76] p. 78. So far as I can tell, the first writer to describe evil as "raw material" for the production of good was H. Wheeler Robinson in *Suffering, Human and Divine* (1940). Hodgson owed much to Robinson's book. However, Robinson, an Old Testament scholar, seems to have thought of suffering as a mysterious way of redemption generally, along the lines of the suffering servant of Isaiah 53, rather than as an ingredient in forgiveness particularly.

[77] p. 64.
[78] p. 78.
[79] p. 13.
[80] p. 83.
[81] p. 83.
[82] p. 150.
[83] p. 149.
[84] pp. 84–85.
[85] p. 84.
[86] pp. 137–138.
[87] p. 70.
[88] p. 56.
[89] p. 57.
[90] p. 57.
[91] p. 55.
[92] p. 55.
[93] pp. 75–76.
[94] pp. 76–77.
[95] p. 77.
[96] p. 78.
[97] p. 79.
[98] pp. 64–65.
[99] p. 65.
[100] p. 43.
[101] p. 43.
[102] p. 43.
[103] p. 115.
[104] p. 118.

[105] I believe that Hodgson borrowed this analysis of evil from C. C. J. Webb; see *Problems in the Relations of God and Man*, pp. 267ff.

[106] It is now becoming almost a commonplace for theologians to say that forgiveness is costly. A recent writer who accepts costly forgiveness and who has made an enormous effort to show how forgiveness is the only atmosphere in which the spiritual life of mankind can flourish is John Austin Baker. His winsome book, *The Foolishness of God* (Atlanta: John Knox Press, 1970, 1975), shows that his theology is in many ways similar to Hodgson's. Though his work is stronger than Hodgson's on the Old Testament background, for example, it does not take the matter of costly forgiveness beyond the place where Hodgson left it in 1951.

5
Cruciform Forgiveness

The Thesis of This Book

Throughout his earthly life Jesus experienced things we are familiar with in our lives, including negative things like temptation, fatigue, and sadness. He also experienced cruelty; he was unjustly condemned, tortured, and executed. And he was raised out of death by God. What is the meaning of all this? I believe that God in Christ accepted suffering as his way of forgiving the men whose sins caused him to suffer. He went to all that trouble and experienced all that pain in order to call men to himself for forgiveness. The experiences of Christ are the measure of God's costly forgiveness of sinners. That is the thesis of this book.

In presenting this theory, I am using as my model for the cross the human experience of costly forgiveness. This human experience is so familiar to us that it has become a truism to say, "Forgiveness is always costly." The familiarity and plausibility of this idea make it an excellent model for explaining the meaning of Christ's death. What we have to do now is carefully to employ this model so that it will illuminate what Christ did. We will begin by stating as precisely as we can the relationship between suffering and forgiveness.

1. Suffering is not so much a preparation for forgiving as

it is the shape or form of forgiving. When someone wrongs you, you do not suffer in order to earn the right to forgive him. It is rather that your forgiveness is best understood in terms of what it costs you.

There are several advantages to speaking in this way. If we are asked, "What does God have to do in order to be prepared to forgive?" it is difficult to give an unambiguous answer. If we answer, "Nothing," we seem to have left no place for Jesus' sacrifice. If we say, "Jesus had to die," we either imply that Jesus' sacrifice made it right for God to forgive whereas it would have been wrong for God to forgive if Jesus had not died, or else we imply that God did not love men enough to forgive them but Jesus' sacrifice purchased God's love for sinners, or both.

Clearly this will not do, and that is why it is better to speak of Jesus' sacrifice as constituting divine forgiveness rather than preparing for it. When the question about preparation for forgiveness is asked, it should be answered with another question: "What do you mean by divine forgiveness? Indulgence, forgetting that men are sinners, withholding punishment—or the costly reconciliation with sinners which we see at the cross?" So we will speak of the cross as determinative of forgiveness. That idea is basic, though at times our phrasing may be susceptible to other interpretations.

This means that forgiveness is not to be confused with indulgence, which costs nothing. It also means that there are different kinds of forgiveness, less costly kinds and more costly kinds.

The same idea may be put another way. If someone asks, "What do you mean by forgiveness?" the best answer I know of is to say, "This is what I have experienced at the hands of those whom I am now accepting." It is how I have hurt as I was wronged that stamps my forgiveness with its most distinctive character.

2. This model is taken from the context of interpersonal relationships. It has nothing in it of the legal, ritual, or eschatological settings, for example. In costly forgiveness, we are dealing with two persons, the offender and the offended. We are saying that the offended person may find it a very painful experience to be wronged, and his bearing of that pain is the most important factor in his forgiveness of the wrongdoer.

The context of interpersonal relationships is not the only one we might use to speak of the atonement of Christ, of course, but it seems to me to be the best one. Since the Christian view of God is that he is personal, it seems appropriate to understand the relationship between God and man by using as a model the relationship of one human being to another.

However, I cannot prove that this is the best setting for speaking of the atonement, or even that it is a good setting. Some people may not find it helpful. For example, if you do not think of God as personal, naturally you will not find it satisfying to speak of Christ's work in terms of interpersonal relationships. Or, you may feel that though God is personal, the interpersonal relationships of human beings do not have enough breadth and depth to allow for a full view of the atonement. Or, you may be reluctant to use this model because you feel it will lead into psychological questions which confuse rather than clarify the theological issues which need to be understood.

You must decide for yourself whether or not a theory of atonement in terms of interpersonal relationships will satisfy you. But it is in these terms that most people live most of their ordinary lives most of the time. In this sense, it is a natural way for us to think of God. But that does not prove that thinking in terms of interpersonal relations is good; it proves only that it is popular. We must decide whether or not we find it satisfying. I do. In fact, I find the interpersonal way of understanding atonement so compelling that I wonder how Christian faith can be understood in any other way. But again I repeat, that is a decision each one must make for himself.

Another objection to the model we have chosen is that it is imperfect because all men are sinners. It is not right, one might argue, to understand God's forgiveness in terms of man's forgiveness since God is righteous, but every human act of forgiveness is done by one who is himself a sinner. This is true. But if we do not use human models for understanding the cross, then of course we shall have to use no models at all, and that means we will understand nothing about Christ's death.

What we must do is to bracket out from our human model the fact that the one who is offended is himself also an offender. We may simply think in terms of a person who has done little or no wrong, but who has been nevertheless profoundly betrayed by another. The model, like all models, is not perfect, but it is true as far as it goes.

Another objection to employing the model of costly forgiveness is that there are human experiences of forgiveness which are not costly. Sometimes it is easy and natural to forgive another person. Surely it must be like that for God.

I recognize that there are situations in which it is not costly to forgive another. For example, there are times when the offender repents even before the offended person is aware of the offense, with the result that the offended person has no opportunity to experience the pain of betrayal. But this does not render costly forgiveness an inappropriate model for the cross. All that matters for our purposes is that there are painful human experiences which result in profound forgiveness, and we find it illuminating to understand the painful experiences of Christ as being like these.

3. In speaking in terms of interpersonal relationships, we accept a number of assumptions that underlie that way of thinking. One is that persons are free to make certain choices. A corollary of this is that they are responsible for the choices they make. Another assumption is that in their relationships with other persons, men sometimes make choices that are bad or wrong. These choices alter their relationship with those whom they wrong, and they leave them separated. What the offender needs in this situation is forgiveness.

I do not intend to defend these assumptions for the simple reason that they are assumptions we all make most of the time. I simply affirm that they apply between God and men as well as between one man and another.

However, in using costly forgiveness as a model for understanding Christ's work, I have made two assumptions which are not ordinary ones for most people and which do need to be explained. They concern God's impassibility and incarnation.

The Impassibility and Incarnation of God

1. One of the presuppositions of this book concerns the impassibility of God. The idea that God cannot suffer is associated with philosophy rather than with religion because in religion God is thought of as personal and personal life is characterized by feeling. So in the Bible God is said to feel joy and anger, for example. Nevertheless, Christians have traditionally affirmed that God is impassible.

But the tendency in recent theology has been to drop the doctrine of impassibility. It is clear that Bushnell, Mackintosh, and Baillie, in their stress upon the costliness of forgiveness, either gave up or drastically revised the doctrine. It is essential to the understanding of atonement as costly forgiveness that God himself experiences the pain that sin brings as a part of his forgiveness of sinners.

Yet at least one theologian of costly forgiveness, Leonard Hodgson, tried to maintain some of the old doctrine of God's impassibility. In my judgment he was correct in this effort, for there is *some* truth in the doctrine.

The truth which the doctrine of impassibility affirms is that God is free.[1] If we are going to insist that forgiveness was costly to God, we especially need to insist that the cost was one which God voluntarily bore. I am persuaded that God is free, that he freely chooses to love men, for example. I also believe that he is free, if he so chooses, to suffer as a way of forgiving men of their sin. That, I am convinced, is what he has done, in Christ.

This is not to say that God never suffered before Christ. Perhaps he did. We shall shortly examine what was new about the incarnation and Christ's sufferings. Our point right now is that whatever God experienced of suffering, either apart from or as a part of the incarnation, he experienced because he freely chose to do so. Nothing was forced upon him, nothing caught him by surprise, and nothing slipped out of his control. When he suffered for men's sins, it was a voluntary suffering, which makes it so much more a matter of sheer grace. This has decisive implications, as we shall see, for our understanding of the necessity of the cross.

So, any experience other than his eternal life of joy is one into which God enters voluntarily, not by coercion. The experience of God with which we are most concerned in this book is his experience of life as a man, as Jesus of Nazareth.

2. Traditionally the meaning of the incarnation was not

stated, as I have done, in terms of an experience of God. The best known statements of the incarnation are the ones devised by the Councils of Nicea and Chalcedon. They taught that Christ was one person in two natures, the divine nature and human nature being uniquely united in him. This explanation was doubtless satisfying to people who thought and spoke in terms of natures, as we said when we discussed Athanasius. It is not so satisfying today, simply because it is foreign to us. We find it more natural to think of someone as a human being, not because he partakes in a mysterious way in a transcendent reality called human nature, but because he is a self who experiences a finite life, as we do, within the limits of our world, history, and culture. A human being makes various kinds of conscious and unconscious responses to this world, including moral, intellectual, aesthetic, and interpersonal responses. Therefore, when we think of Jesus as true God and true man, we naturally think of God as having somehow accepted and experienced this kind of human life once in the history of our world, in Jesus Christ, in the first century, in Palestine.

This incarnation was possible just because God was free. He freely chose to dwell among men, to live this human life, and to participate as an insider in the human experience. He came to know human life, not as an outsider with very sensitive sympathy, but as an insider, and this was a new experience in God's life. The incarnation, so understood, qualifies forever God's relationships with men. He addresses men, judges them, forgives them, and so on, precisely as one who knows from the inside what it is to be a human being.

In this book we are concerned about the meaning of Jesus' sacrifice of himself. That experience, like all the experiences of his incarnate life, forever qualifies God's relationships with man. In particular, it qualifies the nature of divine forgiveness. God does not forgive men now as a distant untouched spectator might forgive them. Rather he forgives them as an involved participant who has suffered because of their sins. In fact, it would be proper to say that God now forgives as only an involved participant can forgive.

We can perhaps make this clearer with a brief story. In time of war an idealistic pastor might urge his people to adopt an attitude of forgiveness towards the people with whom his country is at war. He might support his plea with the teachings of Jesus that we are to love even our enemies. Yet that same minister might well find it nearly impossible to forgive, for example, his own unmarried daughter for becoming pregnant.

It is not that the minister was insincere about forgiveness when he urged his people to forgive their enemies. Not at all. It is just that to forgive a distant people is an altogether different matter from forgiving one who is close to us. The difference is best understood in terms of the pain which the minister feels. The enemies of his country cause him very little pain, so great is his distance from them, but his daughter causes him great pain just because she is his daughter and is close to him. Even though we use the same word *forgiveness* to describe his stance toward enemy armies and the stance he unfortunately failed to take toward his daughter, we are talking about different realities.

This could be expressed by saying that if the minister were more incarnate in the war, as he was in the life of his daughter, he would find that forgiveness of the enemies of his country was not the same thing it had been when he was securely located far away from the battlefield. It would be a different forgiveness because it was qualified by his being incarnate in the battle.

Likewise, God's forgiveness of men is distinctively qualified because he was incarnate in the human experience. Because God was in Christ, divine forgiveness is a forgiveness that has been realized at great cost. It is costly forgiveness. The cost to God of forgiving man was the cross, and so we shall refer to God's forgiveness as cruciform. It is forgiveness which has taken on the form of a cross.

This is not to say that God did not forgive before Christ. He certainly did forgive; the prophets made that clear. Nor is this to say that God's forgiveness of the Jewish people was without its cost to God. Hosea's message was that God's forgiveness of Israel cost God dearly.

Nevertheless, the divine forgiveness which comes to the world in Christ is distinctive. If I may risk sounding irreverent, Christian forgiveness is God's first forgiveness as incarnate, God's cruciform forgiveness. Never before had God forgiven in just this way, at precisely this cost. Never before had man the sinner caused God just this pain. The forgiveness joyously affirmed by the prophets was wonderful; the forgiveness painfully achieved by the Son was more wonderful still.

Before we say more about what made Christian forgiveness so distinctive, I want to call attention to the fact that this understanding of forgiveness binds together indissolubly the person and work of Christ. There can be no thought of separating who he was from what he did, for only if he was God incarnate does cruciform forgiveness have any meaning at all. Cruciform forgiveness is incarnate forgiveness at its highest pitch.

From this it follows that the death and dying of Jesus are one piece with the rest of his historical life. As God incarnate, all of his human experiences contribute to the distinctive quality of divine forgiveness. God's forgiveness of men is what it is not only because Jesus was crucified but also, for example, because God in Christ experienced the human experiences of temptation and of obedience to the law, and of personal friendships with people like Peter. In other words, God was present with those who needed his forgiveness, incarnate among them, as Jesus. Jesus' entire life qualifies forever the divine forgiveness as incarnate forgiveness.

But to say this is not to minimize the final experiences of Jesus' historical life. Just as suffering distinctively qualifies human forgiveness, so it distinctively qualifies divine forgiveness.

The Objectivity of Cruciform Forgiveness

Now we must deal with one of the most important and yet most difficult aspects of any doctrine of atonement, the aspect of objectivity. How are we to understand the divine, incarnate forgiveness as an objective matter? I am convinced that unless we speak of an objective work of Christ, something essential will be lost from the gospel. For the gospel surely means that something objective has been done which is good news for men. It would hardly be good news otherwise.

No modern writer has spoken more forcefully of the objectivity of Christ's work than James Denney. Here is his definition of objectivity: "Reduced to its simplest expression, what an objective atonement means is that but for Christ and His Passion, God would not be to us what He is." [2] This describes the parameters of objectivity: if we understand the cross as constitutive of God's being toward men, our view of atonement is objective.

However, Denney's definition is ambiguous. It does not tell exactly what aspect of God's being toward men was constituted by the cross. Clearly God's entire being was not constituted by the cross. For example, God did not come to love men because of the cross. Denney rejected this idea, as have most theologians. The opposite is true: because God loved men, Christ died for them.

Therefore we ask, what aspect of the being of God toward men was constituted by the cross? I believe that the answer is forgiveness. "But for Christ and His Passion, God would not be [forgiving] to us" in exactly this way. Christian forgiveness is what it is because of Christ and his passion.

We may put the same idea the other way round by asking, In reference to what was Christ's work objective? Was it objective with reference to God's honor, as Anselm said, a payment made to satisfy the honor of God? Or was it objective with reference to God's justice, as Calvin said, a substitute accepting the punishment due to others? Or was it objective with reference to demonic and evil forces, as Aulen said, a victory won over them which liberated mankind from their grasp?

The answer is that the cross understood as costly forgiveness was objective with reference to the life of God. In God's own life something objective occurred in Christ. The experience of suffering even to death in order to forgive sinners was at the cross an experience of God, and therefore the definitive quality of his forgiveness is to be found there. God's forgiveness became cruciform forgiveness then and there.

If the objectivity of the cross is located in God's experience, then it is even more objective than the theories of Anselm, Calvin, and Aulen. For the life of God is a more fundamental reality than his honor or his justice or even the demonic forces.

Whenever we speak of the objectivity of the atonement, some people will inquire if we are rejecting the subjective aspect. That is not our intention at all. Let us recall that we began this study by saying that we are trying to understand the relationship between an historical event, the cross, and the Christian experience of forgiveness. We are very concerned about the subjective experience. We believe that the subjective experience of forgiveness is enhanced, not minimized, if we think of Christ's atoning work as objective.

James Denney expressed this fact by a story.

> If I were sitting on the end of a pier, on a summer day, enjoying the sunshine and the air, and someone came along and jumped into the water and got drowned 'to prove his love for me,' I should find it quite unintelligible. I might be much in need of love, but an act in no rational relation to any of my necessities could not prove it. But if I had fallen over the pier and were drowning, and someone sprang into the water, and at the cost of making my peril, or what but for him would be my fate, his own, saved me from death, then I should say, 'Greater love hath no man than this.' I should say it intelligibly, because there would be an intelligible relation between the sacrifice which love made and the necessity from which it redeemed.[3]

The application to Christ is clear. If by his death Christ somehow objectively rescued men, the subjective appeal of his sacrifice is immense. But if his death was only an attempt to reveal, symbolize, or demonstrate the divine love, it fails even to do that. The objective work of Christ is essential if his death is to have a subjective appeal.

We may express this in terms of our model by saying that since the experiences of Christ were really experiences in the divine life, and since these costly experiences objectively constitute God's way of forgiving sinners, it is perfectly intelligible to speak of the enormous subjective appeal of Christ's sacrifice. Men are profoundly moved to learn that God has forgiven them in this objective, costly way.

Now we shall try to spell out more fully what we mean by

objectivity. One reason it is difficult to understand the objectivity of Christ's work is that objectivity is not a single idea.
It is a cluster of more or less loosely related ideas. What is
needed is a clear analysis of these ideas. The cluster includes
the four following ideas: (1) God did something apart from
any response of men; (2) what God did was new; (3) the new
thing which God did was final; (4) the new, final thing God
did was necessary. We shall discuss these four and see how
each is to be understood when we are thinking about the
cross as costly forgiveness.

1. God did something in Christ which was an achievement apart from any response of men. What he did was to
accept and suffer the consequences of human sin, thereby
qualifying the way in which he accepts repentant sinners.
His forgiveness of sinners is cruciform forgiveness. The sinner who repents receives cruciform forgiveness; he does not
in any way contribute to it. It is already there, as it were,
waiting for him. And it is there because God, incarnate in
Christ, has been crucified.

The same thing is true in human experience. A man who
has been grievously hurt by the betrayal of a friend can
accept his suffering in such a way as will qualify his forgiveness. When the one who offended him and hurt him repents,
he will find forgiveness ready and available. The sinner can
contribute nothing to it. He can only receive what is already
there. And it is there precisely because the man he betrayed
has suffered so deeply. As Bushnell said, if you have accepted the sufferings someone has wickedly caused, "the
forgiveness is in you potentially complete, even though it
should never be actually sealed upon the offender." [4]

This aspect of Christ's objective work has been presented
in various ways through the years. Perhaps the most popular
of these is to use commercial terms. Just as one man may pay

off the debt of another man without any assistance from him, so, it has been said, Christ paid off man's debt. "You are bought with a price," said the apostle Paul.

Commercial terms like *price, transaction,* and *debt* are very helpful provided we do not take them too literally. In that case they would mislead us. We do not ask with whom God made the transaction or from whom God purchased man. In particular, we do not ask how large a price Christ paid for man. Sometimes that was done in the past. For example, Anselm spoke of Jesus' death as being something which, unlike his obedience, he did not owe the Father and therefore something extra which could be applied to the accounts of men (supererogation). Following Calvin's death, Calvinists engaged in debates about whether Christ's death was an atonement limited to saving the elect or an unlimited atonement of value for all the world.

Within the models of Anselm and Calvin, these quantitative ideas may have been appropriate. They are not appropriate in the model of costly forgiveness. There is no room in this theory for formally measuring the cost of costly forgiveness. What we must do is to say, "God's forgiveness is forgiveness whose distinguishing characteristic is that Christ went to the cross as a consequences of the sins which are forgiven."

The first sense, then, in which Christ's work is objective, is that it was done by God apart from any human assistance or response. Thus has God forgiven men.

2. The second sense of the objectivity of Christ's work is that it was a new act of God. This is true in the human model as well. A man may have often forgiven others in various ways. But if on a certain day he suffers in a particularly poignant way as a consequence of another's sin, then on that day he has done something new. The fact that he had forgiven

in other ways at other times does not in the least affect the newness of his achievement on that day.

The same is true of God. He forgave sins long before Christ, as Hosea made clear. Nevertheless, what he did in Christ was a new thing. Never before had God been incarnate, with all that that meant. Never before had God experienced what he experienced in Christ, all the way to the crucifixion itself. All of this was a first experience, a fresh new act of God.

It is quite appropriate to see continuity between the Old Testament and the New, between God's love for Israel and for the church, and between the forgiveness revealed in the teachings of Hosea and in the teaching of Jesus. But there is discontinuity as well. Christian forgiveness is forgiveness by God who is incarnate, not a spectator, not even a sympathetic spectator. And Christian forgiveness is forgiveness by a God who, incarnate as Jesus of Nazareth, experienced terrible pain as a consequence of the sins of the people he came to forgive. So Christian forgiveness is not just any forgiveness; it is cruciform forgiveness. That means that it is a new work of God.

In order to understand the newness of God's act of forgiveness in Christ, we must take seriously its historical character. The suffering of Christ was not merely the revelation of an eternal principle or of an eternal reality. It was an event in history. Whereas one would hardly describe any eternal reality as new, each event in history is new, and the cross was such an event. If God really invaded history in Christ, that was new, new for history and new for God. If God in Christ really experienced the consequences of sin in that painful way, that too was new, new for God. And if this event really qualifies his forgiveness of men, then that forgiveness was also new.

God's cruciform forgiveness is fresh and new because it is a forgiveness whose distinctive characteristic is that it has been wrought in the historical event of incarnation and crucifixion.

3. Third, the new thing which God did apart from any response of men is a finished thing. It had about it a quality of completeness, of something accomplished because it was something done. This is true of human forgiveness. When a man has been betrayed, he can accept the pain of his betrayal in a way that is so final and complete that the betrayal no longer constitutes a barrier between himself and his betrayer. When the offender repents, he may then receive a forgiveness that is complete, full, and perfect, because the man he betrayed has completely, fully, and perfectly accepted the painful consequences of the betrayal. His bearing the consequences of sin so completely means, in effect, that the sin no longer constitutes a barrier between himself and the sinner. Nothing needs to be added to his full acceptance of the suffering that grew out of the sins committed against him.

This is also true of God. In Christ he experienced the painful consequences of sin fully, and therefore finally, by his suffering and death. There is nothing that could be added to the work of Christ. Sin no longer constitutes a barrier between God and man, so fully did God bear its consequences in Christ. Because divine forgiveness is cruciform, it is final.

The finality of cruciform forgiveness, like its newness, rests on the fact that it occurred in history. If, for example, Jesus had merely revealed the costliness of an eternal forgiveness, his work could not be said to be final. This happens to have been the view of Bushnell, but I believe Leonard Hodgson was much closer to the truth. Jesus did not

merely symbolize an eternal suffering of God; he was God
accepting a historical suffering which constituted the distinctive quality of divine forgiveness.

To take another example, Jesus was not merely applying
an eternally true principle when he died. I am not even sure
that it is wise to speak of a principle of costly forgiveness. In
any case, if Jesus had been simply applying a principle, there
would have been nothing final about what he did, since it is
the nature of principles that they are applied repeatedly. But
Jesus was not merely applying an eternal principle. He was
once and for all accepting into his own life all the consequences of human sins, and in so doing he once and for all
determined that divine forgiveness is distinctly cruciform
forgiveness. Once divine forgiveness took this shape, it
forever kept this shape. The only God who forgives sinners is
the God who once became incarnate as Jesus of Nazareth and
who then died at the hands of those sinners. At the cross
divine forgiveness was decisively and finally construed as
cruciform forgiveness and no other.

We have said so far that the cluster of ideas to which we
refer when we say that the atonement is objective includes
three distinctive concepts, that it was God's work apart from
man's response, that it was a fresh, new work, and that it was
a final, complete work.

4. There is a fourth idea that usually appears in the cluster
of ideas we call *objectivity*. My conviction is that it is a
mistaken idea. It is the idea that the cross of Christ was
necessary if God was to save men.

To begin with, we should notice that it is quite possible to
say that the atonement was a new and a final work of God
without saying that it was necessary. In other words, even if
God could have saved men in some other way, the fact is that
this is the way he did save men, and the way that he did save

men was by a new and final act in Christ apart from any effort of men. Necessity may contribute to objectivity, but it is not essential to it.

Second, I admit that in some senses it is appropriate to speak of a necessity for the cross. It was, for example, historically necessary. That is, it was historically inevitable that if Jesus went on pressing his message to Israel, the leaders of Israel would see to it that he was stopped. If nothing else would stop him, they would have him executed. Given the situation in Israel and the way people are, it was inevitable that they would do this. This is not in the least to exonerate them, for men are responsible in large measure for being the kind of persons they are. But when Jesus said that it was necessary for him to suffer many things at the hands of the leaders, I think he meant that it was historically inevitable that he would, and that the disciples were not to be alarmed about this as it too had been taken into account by God.

Another kind of necessity about Christ's death was the necessity of his obedience. He had taught men to put God's kingdom first whatever the cost, and it was necessary for him to do that also, even unto the cross. He had taught men to love God and neighbor. It was necessary for him to do that also, and he did it all the way to the cross. He had taught that we are in an important sense not to resist those who would mistreat us, that we are to forgive our enemies, and that we are to lay down our lives for our friends. When he practiced these things himself, it took him to the cross. In short, it was morally necessary for him to follow his vocation from God, and this took him to the cross. Thus, the cross was necessary in terms of history and in terms of Jesus' vocation.

But that is not what some theologians have meant when they have referred to the necessity of Jesus' sacrifice. They have meant that there is a logical necessity to the cross. They have meant that this was the only route open to God if he intended to save men. That is, in fact, the precise theme of Anselm's book, *Why God Became Man*, as we saw in chapter 3.

Anselm's effort and others like it, however, are misguided because we simply do not know that this was the only way God could have saved men. It is possible that other routes were open to him that we cannot imagine; we just do not know. We must be content, therefore, to say that this is how God *did* save men. We must not try to argue that this was the only way he *could* have done so.

To express this idea in terms of costly forgiveness, we must not say that God could not forgive apart from incarnation and crucifixion. He did it when he forgave Israel in the Old Testament. I do not think it was logically necessary for God to forgive in just the way he did in Christ. Rather, he freely chose to forgive in this costly way. It was an act of freedom, not of necessity.

In our theology we should try to be empirically accurate rather than logically compelling. We ought to be satisfied to say "This is what God has done," without adding, "And this was the only way he could have done it." From the beginning of this book we have been trying to explain what the death of Jesus means; we have not attempted to prove that forgiveness had to happen in just the way it did. Many false turnings in theology can be avoided if we allow our theology to be empirical, simply reporting what God has done, rather than trying to prove that it was necessary that God should have done a particular thing.

To me, it is completely convincing to speak of cruciform forgiveness as a work of God apart from human response, a fresh, new work which he did in history, and a perfect and final work which Christ accomplished once for all. But it is unconvincing to argue that God had to do it in this way. I am satisfied and, in fact, joyously happy, just to say, "Thus has God forgiven us sinners."

NOTES

[1] This is the view of Jurgen Moltmann in *The Crucified God* (London: SCM Press Ltd, 1974). Unlike the theologians of costly forgiveness, however, Moltmann has little interest in the forgiveness of individuals. His real concern is for the political future of mankind.

[2] James Denney, *The Christian Doctrine of Reconciliation* (London: Hodder and Stoughton, 1917), p. 238. Denney made limited use of the model of costly forgiveness in the first half of this book.

[3] James Denney, *The Death of Christ* (London: Hodder and Stoughton, 1909), p. 127.

[4] Horace Bushnell, *Forgiveness and Law*, p. 44.

6
Christ and the Consequences of Sin

We have employed as a theological explanation for Christ's death the model of costly forgiveness taken from the setting of interpersonal relationships. We have argued that God did not have to experience what he did in Christ, but he freely chose to do so. Having become incarnate in Christ, his forgiveness took the shape of a cross. Christ's death was thus objective with reference to the life of God. Forgiving in this way was something God did apart from human response. It was a fresh and new forgiveness, and it was final and complete forgiveness.

In none of this have we isolated Christ's death from his life. Thus, for example, we have spoken of incarnate forgiveness as well as of cruciform forgiveness. Nevertheless, it is appropriate that the final days of Christ's life figure large in the model of costly forgiveness, for it was in those last days that the costliness of his forgiveness reached its climax, and Christ paid the ultimate price.

Therefore, we want now to give particular attention to Christ's suffering and death. Our concern is not the morbid one of knowing the intensity of one aspect or another of his physical or mental torment. Nor is our concern with the emotions Christ may have felt like depression, anxiety, or fear. It is rather the theological one of knowing as much as we can about what sorts of things God in Christ experienced in order to understand better the nature of the forgiveness he provided for men by these experiences.

The usual answer to this is to say that Christ experienced the consequences of sin. This is true, but it is also ambiguous, for sin has different consequences. I want to analyze the consequences of sin in terms of the character of the offended person. We will thus be trying to answer four different questions. First, what consequences of sin does one suffer because one is good? Second, what consequences of sin does one suffer because one loves the sinner? Then, what consequences of sin does one suffer because one is good and loves the sinner? Finally, what consequences of sin does one suffer because one is the victim?

In employing this analysis I risk becoming pedantic, for it is artificial to separate goodness and love. Nevertheless, there is a good reason for doing it. In the history of the doctrine of atonement, confusions and controversies have circulated around these two concepts, and we want to try to sort these out. One asset of the model of costly forgiveness is that it does clarify these questions. I know of no way to be clear about these troublesome issues except to follow at first this rather artificial distinction between love and goodness. In any case, when we answer the third question, we shall be putting the two concepts back together. We shall take up the consequences of sin one by one, in each case first employing a human analogy and then using it to help us understand the experience of Christ.

The Consequences of Sin One Experiences Because One Is Good

Let us assume that you are committed to goodness. When someone commits a terrible sin—say, the murder of the athletes at Munich—it is a severe affront to you. You may not know the sinners, let alone love them, but what they did was such that it causes you pain because you are a good person.

What you feel might be called disgust. Also, in certain instances, you will feel frustration that your good purposes are being thwarted, as would be the case, for example, if you were an ardent supporter of international athletic competition.

The feelings of disgust and frustration are painful to you. This is the first painful consequence of sin to a good person.

It is important to realize that you ought to feel disgust and frustration at such terrible acts. Yet you cannot allow yourself to go on feeling that way indefinitely. So, if you are really good, you will replace your disgust with disapproval of the sin, and your frustration with rejection of the sin. Whereas you had experienced disgust and frustration more or less involuntarily, you adopt the stance of disapproval and rejection quite deliberately. The only alternative to this stance is to give up on the sinner by becoming embittered or indifferent to his being good, or to give up on your good purposes, which would be compromising with sin. Your disapproval and rejection may be understood as punishment.[1] Because you are a good person, this is how you ought to respond to sin. No other option open to you would be as supportive of righteousness as to oppose sin and to help sinners to become righteous.

Disapproval and rejection are the best options open to you under the circumstances, but the fact that wrong has been done prevents you from exercising the best option, which would of course be approval and acceptance. It is second-best to disapprove the sin and dissociate yourself from it.

It hurts you to have to do this, and this is the second painful consequence of sin which a good person feels. It is a costly thing for a good man to have to disapprove of sin and reject it. The father who expresses his disapproval of his child and then says, "This hurts me more than it does you," is usually right.

When you disapprove and reject the sinner, it may be painful for him as well as for you. Of course, he may misread your action. He may feel it as cold justice or even think you hate him. Or he may think your disapproval doesn't matter at all. Whether or not he understands your position may depend on the way you express disapproval and rejection.

You need to express your rejection in a form that communicates your true feeling to him. But even that does not define how disapproval is best expressed. In the case of a child, for example, you may need to express it by scolding then reassuring, or just by spanking, or by depriving him of some privilege until he repents. The essence of a good man's response to sin is disapproval and rejection; how it is expressed is incidental. But experience tells us it is very difficult to express our disapproval so as to communicate accurately our position to the sinner.

Your disapproval may be described as both retributive and reformative. It is retribution in two senses: it is a response to a sin committed, taking into account as much as possible the degree of responsibility of the sinner, and it is expressed in a way and to a degree appropriate to the sin.

Disapproval is moral only if it is deserved, and it is moral only as it is expressed in proportion to the sin committed. Otherwise it is either cruel or indulgent. People assume, because they have seen so much cruelty called punishment, that all disapproval is wrong. They think it is all a matter of lost temper, revenge, sadism, and capricious torture. These objections are legitimate, but the proper response to the abuse of the moral response of disapproval is not to stop it altogether, but to do it properly.

You must disapprove evil if you are to avoid becoming implicated in it. That there are men so committed to the right that they will disapprove of wrong is a hopeful view. If no one cares enough about goodness to oppose evil, things are very bad indeed for everyone.

Disapproval, in the sense we have stated it, is reformative in two senses: its purpose is to lead a man to repentance and so to righteousness, and it is expressed in a way that will do this. This means that you respect the man's freedom, among other things.

Often we find it hard in practice to see how disapproval can be both retributive and reformative. It is difficult to know how to express disapproval of evil that is both appropriate to the wrong done and also that will act upon the wrongdoer so as to contribute to his being improved. But that, surely, is the ideal, as each supports the good in a special way.

In punishing in this way, you have to live with a special tension. This tension has its source in sin, but it exists in you rather than in the sinner. It is the tension of being both against the sinner (because you are for goodness) and for the sinner (in an effort to help him become good).

This tension is the third painful consequence of sin to the offended person: you feel an inner tension in your relationship with the sinner. It is not ambivalence, which is tension arising from being undecided. It is decided: you are both for and against this sinner.

It would be appropriate to call your suffering in all this a consequence of sin. It is also vicarious suffering because he did the wrong but you are hurting.

But what you are experiencing is not punishment. To punish is to disapprove and reject a sinner—it can be done, therefore, only to a sinner. It may look as if you are punishing yourself, since you are experiencing the painful consequences of disapproval and dissociation, and you are living with the inner tension of being both for and against the sinner. Yet it is not punishment; for by definition punishment is done to a sinner, and you feel your pain precisely because you are not a sinner.

When do you withdraw your disapproval of the sinner? There are three possible answers. One is that you withdraw it when the sinner has suffered enough. There is some truth in this. However, your goal is that the sinner become righteous. If he continues not to repent, then he continues to frustrate your purpose, and so he continues to deserve your disapproval.

A second answer is that you withdraw your disapproval when some sort of payment has been made to satisfy goodness. This won't do. The only thing, in an interpersonal context, that can be said in any meaningful sense to satisfy goodness is for the sinner to become a good person. You should continue to disapprove so long as he continues to be evil.

The true answer is that you withdraw disapproval when a man repents and so begins the pilgrimage to goodness.

The same thing is true in terms of the tension you feel in being both for and against the wrongdoer. It cannot cease until the sinner repents, and then it will. Its source is his sin and it continues as long as sin does.

If he repents, what then? You withdraw your disapproval of him. That is the nature of your forgiveness at this point: he is no longer opposed by a good person, but is completely accepted.

It is righteous, not wrong or compromising, to withhold punishment of a repentant person. It will lead to righteousness in the sinner, which means it is righteous.

Some people have minimized the importance of forgiveness as nonpunishment. This is a mistake, for nonpunishment is very important. It certainly feels very important to one who has experienced it.

What is the cost of this forgiveness? It was preceded by costly punishment, costly as disgust and frustration, then as disapproval and rejection, and also as inner tension. So the route to forgiveness has been characterized by the bearing of certain painful experiences. It is therefore somewhat costly.

By this analysis, I am suggesting that since God is good, our sin causes him pain in these ways: first as disgust and frustration of his purposes which, second, he transforms into an equally painful disapproval and rejection of us which, third, leaves him with a painful inner tension in that he is both for and against us.

His rejection and disapproval are right; that is how he ought to respond to sin. It is the best option open to God. But it is still a second-best matter, since to have a good man would have been better. His rejection is painful for the sinner, or can be made so, which may lead the sinner to assume, quite wrongly, that God hates him. God's disapproval is retributive and reformative in character.

Here I need to add that it is a personal response in a context of interpersonal relationships. It is not legal: our concern throughout has been for God's purposes of goodness, not for legal standards.

Nor is God's disapproval impersonal. For various reasons, people have regarded it as such. They say sin is its own worst punishment, or that there is a mechanism built into nature which sees that sin reaps what it has sown. A liar loses credibility, a selfish person is locked into a world of his own, alone, and greedy men experience profound dissatisfaction with all they possess. Clearly, there is much truth here. But it is not what we are talking about.

What we are talking about is God's personal response to

sin. We want to stay in the realm of personal relationships. The impersonal reflexes of the world are realities; they may even serve as the mechanism by which God's personal disapproval of evil is expressed. But they do not displace God's personal reaction to man's sin. It, too, is a reality with which we ought to be concerned.

This divine disapproval continues until men repent. That is proper. There can be no buying off of it, of course.

When a sinner repents, God withdraws his disapproval. This is the forgiveness of God as righteous. Forgiveness in this sense is an appropriate response to man's repentance. The second-best divine response to sin, punishment, is replaced by the best when a man starts via repentance on the road to becoming a good man. It is far more important, and more supportive of righteousness, that sinners are transformed into good men than that each sin is disapproved indefinitely.

When God forgives a man in this sense, having borne the pain which he did, it is a great thing. One who has experienced it will rejoice in it: "God no longer condemns me! What joy!"

This might be the whole story. It certainly is a great story. If sin were only a frustration of God's purposes and not also a betrayal of his person; if God awaited our repentance and did nothing to induce us to repent; if God were righteous toward us but not loving toward us, then this would be the whole story.

But we have betrayed God; he does help us to repent; he does love us. So there is something more to be said about forgiveness.

The Consequences of Sin One Experiences Because One Loves the Sinner

If someone you love wrongs you, your experience cf the

consequences of his sin will be profoundly affected by your love. It will be far more painful than what a righteous man experiences.

The following list is not comprehensive, but it indicates some of the range of what a lover may experience.

(a) A wife whose husband sins may well experience a profound sense of shame. This is because she is so closely identified with him. This is the phenomenon which gives credibility to Campbell's idea of vicarious repentance: the husband sins; it is his wife who is ashamed.

(b) A parent whose child turns against all that the parent believes in and goes his own way and renounces his parents will feel a profound sense of loss.

(c) A man may be forsaken by his sweetheart, who betrays all their mutual commitments and scorns him. He will certainly feel a sense of betrayal.

(d) A friend who watches his friend turn against him may see with great clarity that the route his friend has chosen will lead to his destruction. He will therefore experience a deep sadness because of the fate of his friend. This experience is virtually identical to the empathy of which Don Browning spoke: he hurts for the pain which his friend is causing himself.

All of these experiences are painful. You feel this sort of pain because you love and are concerned for the welfare of the one you love.

The only way you can avoid this pain is to stop loving the sinner. This may not be easy, but you could cultivate indifference, move away from him, turn all your attention elsewhere. Eventually you might do it. Leonard Hodgson said the only alternative to pain of this kind is bitterness. I think he was wrong; indifference is possible. In some cases, it might even happen without your effort. You might just cease to care.

If you determine to keep loving, that entails your accepting pain like shame, loss, betrayal, and sadness. For this reason, you almost certainly will have to make a deliberate decision if you are to continue to love. Loving is costly when it is a sinner you love, because his sin causes pain to anyone who loves him.

Your bearing this cost will help the sinner to repent. If he sees how he has hurt you, it may well encourage him to turn from sin. It may lead him to trust you to forgive him as well as to turn from his sin. For if you have borne this kind of pain for him, that is a sure sign that you will be willing to forgive him.

Forgiveness here is more than the forgiveness of a good man, for it has been made possible at greater cost. If you had not accepted the shame, loss, betrayal, sadness, and so on, you would have ceased loving and so would have been in no position to forgive even if the sinner repented. You would have been indifferent, as we said. In short, your very wonderful forgiveness of a repentant sinner you love takes its shape and form from the painful experiences his sin costs you just because you love him. In this it is greater than forgiveness provided by the good man, whose pain (disapproval, rejection, and tension) was less.

Your suffering was vicarious. It was close to vicarious repentance, though not identical to it. And it was identical with psychotherapeutic empathy. However, it was not vicarious punishment, though both you and the sinner might say things that could be interpreted that way. He might say, for example: "I treated my wife so badly I deserved to suffer; and yet she suffered. She suffered for me." All of this is true. But if punishment is disapproval and rejection of a sinner by a good person, she did not suffer that, for she was not the sinner in this case.

Further, we should not think of the suffering as a way of purchasing love. It may look very much like that, but it is not. It is only because love was present to begin with that one would accept this kind of pain.

By this analysis I am suggesting that since God loves men who are sinners, their sin causes him pain like the human pain of shame, loss, betrayal, and sadness. He continues to love them, which means the pain goes on for him. This is how his forgiveness is distinctively qualified, by the cost he bore to provide it. It was Bushnell's great contribution that he made this so clear.

We are now talking about divine costly forgiveness. We find this not only in the Christian message but also in the Jewish prophets, especially Hosea.

It has been an artificial thing to isolate the pain of a good person from that of a loving person. We must now give attention to how these two are related. The problem is that people often assume that they conflict, the demand for goodness requiring us to punish while the concern of love leading us to show mercy. We shall have to ask if that is an accurate picture of what a man who is both good and loving experiences when he is sinned against.

The Consequences of Sin One Experiences Because One Is Good and Loves the Sinner

Let us begin with an example. A betrayed husband may suffer many things because of his wife's infidelity. He may feel disgust at her wantonness and a sense of frustration at his purpose to share a happy marriage with her. If so, he must either give up his purpose, which is a compromise at best, or else give up on her, which means being embittered toward her. Or else he must transform his disgust into disapproval and his frustration into a kind of rejection of wantonness, including his wife's wantonness. To do this he will have to live with very great inner tension which is painful for him, the tension of being altogether for his wife yet completely opposed to her infidelity. Furthermore, because he loves her, he is ashamed at her infidelity, he feels a loss in her leaving him, he feels profoundly betrayed, and he feels very sad to see her embark on a course that he knows will cause her continual misery and will eventually destroy her.

If he can accept all this pain—the pain of rejecting and disapproving, the pain of inner tension of being both for and against her, the pain of shame, loss, betrayal, and sadness—then he can continue to be both good and loving toward his wife. And if she then repents, she will find waiting for her a husband whose forgiveness is profound and rich. It will include the fact that he no longer opposes her. But more than that, it will be a costly forgiveness characterized by his having borne such painful experiences as these for her.

The question is: Is there a tension between love and goodness in the life of a husband like this? The answer is: There is not.

1. For one thing, love and goodness have much in common. Both have been painful experiences. Both have as their purposes the sinner's repentance, and both are in his interest. Punishment is loving in that it acted to reform and respected the sinner's freedom. Costly forgiveness is good in that it is the best hope the sinner has for becoming righteous. And it is good to suffer in order to forgive another.

2. The second reason that we think that there is no tension between love and goodness is that the tension is already experienced by the one who is good. Precisely as good and to support goodness, one must both oppose a sinner and be for him: oppose him so as not to compromise with his sin yet be

for him so as to allow him to become good. Further, there is the same kind of tension in one who loves; for he is for the sinner and yet, for that very reason, opposed to what the sinner is doing that is self-destructive.

The tension then is not between love and goodness. There is no tension between grace and righteousness or between mercy and justice. The tension is within righteousness itself and within love itself. The difficulty is not how to be both good and loving. It is how to be good, which means you are both for and against the sinner. And it is how to be loving, which means you are both against and for the sinner. The ideal, certainly, is somehow to express both your good, loving opposition and your good, loving acceptance.

Further, the tension a man feels does not have its source in his goodness or his love. The source of the tension is always the sin. If there were no sin, a good man would feel no tension, nor would a loving man.

Further, there can be no thought of relieving the tension except by the sinner's repentance, forgiveness, and transformation. A good, loving man does not relieve the tension by accepting some special suffering, arbitrary or not. Indeed, the tension is causing him suffering, and he must continue to bear this in order to be good *and* loving.

In this analysis we are again saying something about God. He is both good and loving. From this it follows that he experiences both types of suffering we have been describing. And his forgiveness is both the withdrawing of punishment and the more costly acceptance of one who loves.

Also, God experiences the tension of goodness, as both opposing sin and supporting the sinner, and the tension of love, as being both for the sinner and against what is destroying him. But this tension is not between love and righteousness at all, for the reasons given above. Nor can it be relieved except upon the repentance of the sinner. There must be no talk of buying God's love or of buying off his righteousness or of relieving God of the tension. It endures until the sinner is reconciled and goodness prevails.

We have tried to make it clear how costly forgiveness is to God because he loves. This is truly a wonderful word: God loves sinners so much that he will suffer whatever is involved to forgive them. It is a word of grace, of joy, and of hope for the human predicament. Little wonder there is rejoicing in heaven over one sinner who repents, for it means that God has not suffered in vain.

In accepting these sufferings in this way, God not only has forgiven but he has also helped the sinner to repent. He did this in part by his firm stand against sin, which may shock a sinner awake to the enormity of his evil. But he did it even more by paying the price involved in suffering the consequences of sin to love. He revealed all this to men through Hosea and others, and this is a very great help to them. Surely this revelation will shame them to repentance and foster in them trust in God.

What a glorious message this is. What a marvelous thing, this costly forgiveness. And yet, for all that, it is not God's final word. For there is another sense in which God has experienced the consequences for human sin: he has been the victim of sin. To this astonishing fact we now turn our attention, for, like the other consequences of sin, it too defines the divine forgiveness.

The Consequences of Sin to One Who Is a Victim

We are arguing that we understand the meaning of forgiveness by seeing what experiences the forgiver has had en route to forgiving the sinner. So we must deal with a very obvious consequence of sin which some people experience en route to forgiveness, namely, that they have themselves been the victim of the sin. Of course, it might be said that in a sense all good people are victims of any sin or that anyone who loves a sinner is a victim. But I am referring to the more narrow use of the word. A victim of theft is a man who has been robbed. A victim of rape is a woman who has been assaulted. A victim of child-abuse is a battered child.

We usually assume that people are involuntarily victimized. They cannot do anything about their suffering, like the citizen who is abused by a vicious government or the hapless bank clerk who is shot during a robbery. But there is such a thing as a voluntary victim. It is rare, and there are difficulties associated with it, but it is meaningful; people do sometimes voluntarily become victims of sin.

A voluntary victim is a person who is so removed from a sin that he is not involuntarily one of its victims. Perhaps he is geographically so far away that the sin cannot reach him. Perhaps he is so shrewd that he cannot be touched by the sin, or so powerful that the sin cannot reach him. In any case, he is secure. He may suffer as a good man does at sin and even suffer as a loving man does at sin, but he is not in a place to become the victim of sin.

But he makes a decision; he decides to become vulnerable. He moves out of his security to the place where sin is going on and is hurting people. The great difficulty with this concerns his motive. The logical thought is that his motive is unhealthy; he is a masochist who wants or needs to suffer. Sometimes this is the case.

But there is another possibility. Suppose he is a good person who loves the sinner. We have already seen the kind of painful experiences that sin costs a good, loving person. And we have seen how much help he provides to the sinner by bearing these experiences. But suppose he wants to do more and to try even harder to recall the sinner. Is any route open to him?

There is. If he has been shielded from being a victim, he can express his goodness and love, his costly punishment and costlier forgiveness, by going into the situation where sin is, by foregoing his security. He can reinforce all that he has already done for the sinner simply by being present himself rather than safely sending a message of the pain he has borne in his isolated invulnerability.

This is an acceptable, healthy motive for becoming a voluntary victim. We can deny this only if we do not, or cannot, believe that such love could exist. We would not have to be entirely cynical to do this, since it does stretch our imagination to suppose that any healthy person could be this altruistic, unselfish, and self-sacrificing. Yet it can happen, and it does.

We are talking now about something more than the pain of disapproval, the tension of goodness, shame, loss, betrayal, and sadness, and all the rest of it. We are talking now of a new kind of experience, the experience of voluntarily experiencing victimization.

It is a new experience for the forgiver. He could have been wonderfully forgiving before, but becoming a victim would still be something new.

There is a certain freedom here that was not present in his earlier choices, wonderful as they were. For, as committed to goodness, he more or less had to act as he did in punishment, painful as it was. And in loving the sinner, he more or less had to accept the pain which he did. Only in this way could he go on being good and loving.

But no prior commitment could in any sense require leaving security for vulnerability. The glory of voluntarily risking victimization is precisely that it takes you beyond anything that could be required. It is the extra mile, the act of sheer grace, just because it is completely voluntary.

We might express it like this. A sinner who understood his sin would never feel he had the right to be forgiven. Still, he might think it reasonable that a good man would withdraw his punishment when he repented. And, deeply moved, he should not be surprised that one who loved him and suffered so much because of him would be so forgiving when he repented.

But nothing could have prepared him for one who would voluntarily become his victim in his effort to win him back. It is an act of such sheer, unexpected sacrifice, a forgiveness so incredible that a thoughtful person would feel stunned by it.

The essential freeness of this act makes the resulting forgiveness qualitatively different from the previous forgivenesses, good as they were. Now we are speaking of a forgiveness that is withdrawal of rejection, but it is more. It is a reunion of persons that has been very costly to the forgiver, but it is still more. It is the forgiveness of one who is a victim, but it is more. It is the forgiveness of one who, good and loving, has voluntarily accepted victimization in order to recall the sinner.

There is an ultimate quality about this. In order to help a person repent and become good, in order to be prepared to forgive, in order to be united with the sinner, there is nothing more you can do than put yourself in this vulnerable situation. In doing it, you do all you have previously done, only better. You recall the sinner better, express your disapproval and rejection better, affirm your love better, describe the pain of your shame and betrayal and so on better, by being present than in any other way. No message, no revelations from a secure place, could possibly communicate your love as well as your voluntary vulnerability does.

Once again in this analysis, I am saying something about God. But I am no longer speaking in terms of the Old Testament, or of divine sympathy in heaven, or of prophetic messages, however gracious.

I am now talking in terms of something so astonishing that, if we had not seen it, we could not and would not have believed it. But once in history, we have seen it. In Christ we have seen God accepting the pain our sins cause him as good, but more; accepting the pain our sins cause him as loving us, but more; accepting the pain our sins cause him as our victim, but more: in Christ we have seen God accepting the pain our sins cause him as voluntary victim. He did and does this in order to bring us back to himself.

And it is this experience in the divine life that finally defines God's forgiveness. It is in this way he forgives, and not in any other. God's forgiveness is cruciform. It is the shape of the cross.

We may see more clearly what we mean by God's forgiveness being cruciform if we realize that the word *forgiveness*, like all human words, though it is true when used of God, is not adequate for what he has done. In other words, we should think of the word *forgiveness* as a container, partially filled with meaning by familiar human experiences of forgiveness. But as we begin to use it of God, we must allow the container to receive much of its meaning from God's actions. That is, what God did at the cross defines the meaning of the word *forgiveness* when it is used of God. It is simply wrong to ask, "Why must Christ die if God is to forgive?" That question erroneously assumes that we know exactly what God's forgiveness is. We do not. Rather we should ask, "How, as a matter of fact, has God forgiven men?" That question permits God's act to define the word *forgive*. And the answer to the question is to point to the cross and say: "There. That is how God has forgiven, by bearing those consequences of man's sin. He died on a cross—that is the meaning of the divine forgiveness."

Throughout this chapter we have been assuming that forgiveness leads to a sinner becoming a good person. Now we must justify this assumption by explaining the dynamics of the process of transformation.

NOTES

[1] The word "punishment" is used in this way by, for example, A. C. Ewing in *The Morality of Punishment* (London: Routledge and Kegan Paul, 1929). It is, of course, used in very different senses by others. In particular, it is used to describe the infliction of pain (or withholding of good) upon a criminal in order to express disapproval. All of these usages assume a retributive theory of punishment: it has entirely different uses in any utilitarian theory. Because the word "punishment" is used in various and even contradictory ways, in this book I have used it as little as possible.

7
After Forgiveness

In the two previous chapters, I tried to show that if we understand the sacrifice of Christ in terms of costly forgiveness, we can see a clear and definite connection between Christ's death and resurrection long ago and the experience of a man today who feels that God has forgiven his sins for Christ's sake. I argued, further, that the model of costly forgiveness effectively expresses the objectivity of Christ's work in the very life of God himself. It says everything that has been important to objective theories of atonement with the single exception that it sees the ultimate sacrifice as being an act which God freely chose, rather than one that was in some sense necessary or required of him, as has sometimes been said in the past.

In showing the relationship between Christ's sacrifice and a Christian's being forgiven, I have given my answer to the question which we first set out to answer. Nevertheless, something remains to be said, for we need to understand not only the connection between the cross and forgiveness but also the connection between the cross and a man's becoming a good person. This was, as we saw, the only question which concerned Hastings Rashdall. Also we want to ask, what are the effects of Jesus' sacrifice upon the entire world? Is there a cosmic dimension to redemption?

These are not esoteric questions. It is quite natural for

Christians who see forgiveness as the first step on a long journey to ask where it will lead them and what the cross means for all of God's creation. Our purpose in this chapter is to attempt to answer these two questions.

Cruciform Forgiveness and the Transformation of Persons

Hastings Rashdall sought to discover a direct connection between the cross and the transformation of a man's character. In effect, he bypassed forgiveness because he felt that it could be taken for granted, but the divine forgiveness was far too costly for that. We need to sketch out the connection, which Rashdall and others like Bushnell ignored, between a man's being forgiven and his becoming a changed man. In traditional theological language, we must show how justification leads to sanctification.

Rashdall was certainly correct to be concerned about the transformation of character. It has been the great concern of thoughtful men over the centuries to know how a man can become good. God revealed through the prophets to Israel that what he required of men is not fastidious ritual practices but a high moral quality of life. Nor is this emphasis lost in the New Testament. It would be a fatal perversion of the Christian message to say that God forgives men so freely and fully that there is no motive for them to attempt to become good men. No Christian who understands God's purposes would ever continue in sin that grace might abound. The prophets tied together religion and morality, and the Christian message reinforces the knot.

It is true that in order to make clear that a man cannot make himself righteous before God, Christians have emphasized that salvation is God's work, not man's. This is obvious in forgiveness. But from this it does not follow that

Christians are indifferent to moral transformation. It is true that Augustine resisted the theology of Pelagius who taught that man should cooperate in his own salvation. Since then the church more or less has followed his example. But Augustine was just as concerned as Pelagius that men become good men. The question was not whether men should be transformed but how. Pelagius thought it could be done by human effort. Augustine felt that God must do it by his grace, and that is the line I have taken in this book. God by his grace forgives men, and this is the beginning of their being transformed into good men.

Now let us sketch out in very fundamental terms what we mean by a man being a good man. There are certain phrases which rise naturally to a Christian's mind when he thinks of a good man. A good man is one who loves God with all his heart and loves his neighbor as himself; a good man is one whose faith works by love; a good man is one whose life follows a pattern like that of Jesus, living unselfishly for other men, obedient to his Father. Without suggesting that these phrases are either complete or self-explanatory, and without suggesting that they relieve a man of the need to wrestle with some situations in which the good solution is unclear if indeed there is a good solution, let us accept these phrases as descriptive if not definitive of a good man. We will be content to say that if a man loves God and his neighbor, he will have kept all the law. For our concern is not with the admittedly important question of how a man can know what is good; it is with the even more important question of how God can make good men.

Does it, in fact, mean anything definite to say that one man is good in a sense in which another is not? I believe it does, and I think it can be seen by an illustration. Suppose you handed me a loaded pistol and said to me, "Can you shoot me?" It is an ambiguous question. If you are asking whether I know how to aim the pistol at you, release the safety, and pull the trigger so that you would be hit by the bullet, then the answer is "Yes, I can shoot you."

But if you mean "Are you the kind of person who would shoot me?" the answer is "No, I cannot shoot you." I am the sort of person who is not able simply to fire a gun at another person. Of course, you might think of circumstances in which I could shoot you, such as if my own life were threatened. But that does not alter the situation: under the present circumstances I cannot shoot you, because I am the person I am.

You may say that there are very few persons who could randomly and purposelessly shoot another human being. Fortunately this is true. However, there are some who could do this. I could not. Therefore there is a fundamental difference in my character and theirs.

You may say that it is not very helpful to be the sort of person who does not shoot people. What is needed is that one become the sort of person who does not do any wrong, who always does right. That is, what one needs is to become the sort of person whose character is such that one always loves God with all one's heart and one's neighbor as oneself.

All this is true, but it does not affect my point which is simply that it is meaningful to speak of two men as being different sorts of men, and I have tried to show this by an example. Character is a meaningful concept.

The question is, how can good character be achieved? What does God do to make men into the kind of persons who love him and their neighbor as themselves?

Many things contribute to make a person what he is. For all the modern progress in sociology and psychology, it is quite possible that we do not yet know what most of them are. This is because many of them are acting upon us without our being aware of them.

This is a good thing. I believe that there cannot be any human life that is not influenced by elements in the environment, even though some of these are unconscious influences and some of them are bad. The only alternative to this is for each man to live in complete isolation from other people and from the world. And this is not really an alternative, for complete isolation is itself an environment in the sense that it shapes the kind of person one becomes. In other words, it is inevitable that a man's character is shaped by forces he is not aware of.

I would argue that God employs certain indirect means of transforming men into good persons. To name only two influences, the Jewish-Christian ethic, with its source in the law and the prophets, and the institutional church, have been powerful influences in Western civilization and, in spite of their manifest inadequacies, have shaped the character of millions of persons many of whom rarely if ever think about them.

But there is more to the formation of a man's character than cultural, institutional, and other unconscious influences. For men are what they are in part because of forces of which they are quite aware. Among these none is more powerful than the influence of another person with whom one stands in a close relationship.

Of course, interpersonal influence may be a bad thing. One youth may influence another to enter a life of crime, for example. But it may also be good, and fortunately it often is. Millions of people have had the experience of having a relationship with someone whose influence partially or even radically altered their character for the better.

Interpersonal influence may be exercised by force or coercion. Perhaps, as in the case of parents and small children, there are occasions on which coercion is an appropriate way for one person to influence another. What I want to say here is that there are occasions where coercion is the last way one would ever think of to describe what happened. Rather, one might say: "I would not be what I am apart from Sam, yet never once in all our relationship did he coerce me in any way. So far from coercing me, he influenced me as he did precisely because he respected my freedom."

This, I believe, is the most helpful way of understanding how one person who forgives another can go on to influence the kind of person he is and can become. It is natural that when a man has forgiven another, as their relationship continues, the forgiven man would be affected by the one who had forgiven him. In fact, a forgiving friend is the best hope a sinner has of becoming a better person.

Let us suppose, for example, that a husband is unfaithful to his wife. She suffers enormously as a consequence of his betrayal. He sees her suffering and is deeply moved by it. He recognizes that her stand for fidelity is not merely selfish, and he comes to respect her conviction about it. He realizes from her suffering how much she loves him, and he knows that he can trust her to forgive him. And so he asks for forgiveness and receives it. She no longer rejects him in any sense; they are reconciled.

But that is not the end of the story; for as his actions have shown, this husband is the sort of person who *can* be unfaithful to his wife. Though he has been completely forgiven, he still needs to be transformed. Let us suppose that the wife is not only faithful to her husband but also she is the kind of person for whom it would be unthinkable that she ever would be unfaithful. Marital fidelity is second nature to her. She is that sort of person.

Now, what can she do to assist her husband to become a faithful spouse?

First, we want to admit that there are many unconscious influences in her husband's life other than her own. These may range from seductive and available partners in infidelity, on the one hand, to the powerful influences of the husband's happy childhood with parents who practiced fidelity to each other, on the other hand. But though there are many important, unconscious influences upon the husband, they are not the whole story.

For, like all human beings, he will be influenced by those persons whom he is closely related, and his wife is one of those. Shall she coerce him into fidelity? I will not say that it should never be done; perhaps under some circumstances it should. Nor will I say that it could not be done, for I expect that it probably could. Nor will I say that the distinction between coercive and noncoercive influences is clear. Perhaps it varies from one occasion to another, and making the distinction is more like an art than a science.

What I am saying is that the wife could choose to influence her husband in a noncoercive way. This would keep their relationship a mutually personal one.

If she does make this choice, her forgiveness would play a major role in helping her husband to become faithful. Indeed, I would argue that only if she forgave him, with all the painful experiences which forgiveness involved for her, would she be in a position to exercise this kind of profound personal influence upon him.

Having forgiven him, however, she has gone a long way toward transforming him. Now he will be grateful to her for what she has done, and gratitude will motivate him toward fidelity. In accepting forgiveness, he accepted in principle that his old infidelity was wrong; so he is now operating with new insight into the moral situation. In being forgiven he will have experienced a catharsis, or cleansing, so that he will not feel as irremediably bad as he otherwise might. Because he has seen in his wife's suffering a revelation of her love, he will have a tremendous sense of assurance concerning her. This assurance will support him when his own efforts at fidelity falter and he becomes confused. In being reconciled to his wife, he is united to one who is characterized by fidelity, and this gives him hope which spurs on his efforts at faithfulness. Because he is forgiven he is not alone in his struggle with temptation. He therefore escapes from a vicious cycle of sin and guilt and more sin. Most comprehensively of all, as a forgiven man he participates in the life of a community made up of two persons (which is in turn part of a larger community) which is committed to marital fidelity.

What I want now to suggest is that this is an excellent model for understanding how God transforms men's lives. At the cross God in Christ bore the ultimate consequences of sin, thereby giving shape to divine forgiveness. When a man repents and trusts God, he is gloriously forgiven. This brings him under the conscious noncoercive influence of God. Whatever else God may be doing to transform the man, it is clear that in the setting of interpersonal relationship, forgiveness opens up relationships which lead to the sinner becoming a good man. These would include the man's gratitude, his new moral vision, his sense of being cleansed, his new understanding of God's costly love, the influence of God's love and goodness upon him, and most of all, his participation in the life of God and of God's people. No better hope for a sinner is conceivable, it seems to me, than that he should be forgiven by God in this costly way. If this cannot transform him, I am sure that nothing can.

Does this mean that every forgiven person will eventually become completely good? It is not, I suppose, logically inevitable, but given enough time, it is very natural. The early church joyously affirmed that their sanctification was certain because they were sure that God would go on with this transforming work until it was finished. He who had begun the good work in them would continue it until it was complete (Phil. 1:6). God, having reconciled sinners to himself by Christ's death, would certainly go on to complete their salvation (Rom. 5:10).

It is not our purpose here to sort out the various means by which God brings his personal influence to bear upon Christians. There are many of these, and they are discussed in theology under the heading of means of grace. It seems probable that God would use whatever good means he needs to bring his influence to bear upon a man's life, just as it seems probable that a wife would use any available good means to help her husband become faithful. If this is true, no comprehensive list could in any case be drawn up of the means God uses.

My conviction is that when a man receives God's costly forgiveness, he enters a relationship in which God's personal influence will so shape his life that he will finally become the kind of person who freely loves God with all his heart and his neighbor as himself. If this conviction is correct, then we can go on to inquire about the very difficult subject of the cosmic dimensions of salvation.

The Final Victory of the God of Cruciform Forgiveness

The *Christus Victor* theory of Gustaf Aulen was set in a context of virtually military conflict. For this reason we are unable to assign to it the kind of priority that Aulen did.

And yet we cannot help but ask if there ought not to be a victorious quality to any good theory of atonement, including the theory we are using. I believe that there should be, and I propose to treat the idea of Christ winning a victory over evil as a quality of cruciform forgiveness rather than as a separate theory.

We may begin by speaking of the victory of forgiveness itself. Cruciform forgiveness was victorious over evil in the sense that God in Christ triumphantly bore all the consequences of sin to his goodness and love, even becoming sin's victim, as his way of receiving sinners to himself. Forgiveness was triumphant over punishment in the sense that God righteously withdrew punishment from men when they repented. And it was triumphant over alienation in that it effected the reconciliation of God and man.

Second, cruciform forgiveness was victorious over the moral failure in men's character. Since forgiveness is the indispensable first step on a man's pilgrimage toward becoming a good person, it is proleptically triumphant over moral evil. This is a very important victory as no other contribution toward a transformed world, however grand, can come to anything unless this one occurs. If men are not themselves changed, changing their environment will not in the end amount to much.

Unfortunately, however, these great victories of forgiveness and transformation do not touch the life of most of the world. They are clearly a decisive victory for Christians, but they seem to offer nothing to those who do not accept God's forgiveness and transforming influence.

In the past, Christians have claimed that the work of Christ was cosmic, effecting all the world. This was certainly implied in Peter's gospel of a new age; but, as we saw, Peter did eventually go on to urge people to repent so as to benefit from the forgiveness of the new age.

Can we say anything about a victory of the cross on behalf of those who never receive forgiveness? This is a very difficult question. I want to attempt an answer to it although I know the answer will be incomplete and inadequate.

Let us begin by observing what sort of problems the world has which need to be defeated. How do we today understand the evil forces which are destroying our lives and our world and from which we would pray that God would deliver us?

There are many diagnoses available, but we will look at a few well-known ones. One of the most influential suggestions is that man's basic problem is economic: human ills are all a result of the unequal distribution of wealth caused by greed. The solution to man's problem is the destruction of unjust economic systems.

A second analysis is that man's fundamental problem is ignorance. People behave badly because they are poorly educated. The solution to man's problem is for reason to destroy the evils of ignorance and prejudice by means of education.

A third analysis says that man's basic problem is a loss of heritage. People have lost all sense of history and of their past, and this has resulted in a profound sense of insecurity. People do not feel they really belong. What men need is to recover their roots.

Another suggestion is that modern man has been dehumanized by technology and bureaucracy. He feels like a bit in a machine rather than a person. The solution is the destruction of the dehumanizing factors in modern life.

Another suggestion is that human beings today cannot communicate with one another. They function in a kind of Babel situation, with everyone talking and no one listening. What is needed is to tear down all the barriers that keep people apart.

Yet another solution is that men are afflicted with existential anxiety. They rail against their finitude, and they can find no purpose for their lives, which means their marriages break up, they always feel inadequate, and they are suicidal. The only solution is to overcome their purposelessness.

One other suggestion is that man's problem arises from deep in his unconscious mind. As a result of long-forgotten experiences of his childhood, and perhaps even of experiences in which he never participated, man is a cauldron of conflicting emotions. The solution to all this is for men to come to terms with these vexing emotions.

These seven diagnoses are attempts to specify the root of the human predicament. But the human problem is much more than a matter of underlying causes. For most people most of the time, the dominant concern is for the many effects arising out of these underlying causes. People are hungry, homeless, unemployed, anxious, unloved, frightened, discouraged, confused, suffering, sick, and dying.

Our question is, Did Christ at the cross somehow make provision for the resolution of these problems in the same *direct* way he did for the problem of sin and guilt? I believe that he did not. I cannot see that Jesus died to provide for the special needs of the third world, to provide them with a special strain of rice or an ingenious solution to housing problems. Christ did not reconcile capitalism and communism or educate the illiterate. He did not help urban men to know about their roots or show them how to avoid technolbgy's dehumanizing side effects. His death did not destroy communication barriers, existential anxiety, or psychological slush funds. He did not provide a cure for broken marriages, inferiority complexes, or suicidal tendencies.

This frank admission about the cross and the human predicament may scandalize some Christians. But it seems to me to be true. Now I must add to it some qualifications.

First, Christians face these problems just as other men do, and the Christian experience of forgiveness helps them to cope with them. Let us take two examples. One effect of the human predicament is a sense of being unloved. A man who suffers from this may well find that when he accepts God's forgiveness he begins to feel that God loves him, and as he lives his life in the church he may find that he no longer feels unloved at all.

Again, one of the diagnoses for man's problem is that men are floundering because they have no sense of heritage. A man who accepts God's forgiveness may find that his spiritual heritage meets that human need. He may not know his physical ancestors, but he knows his spiritual ones, and he comes to love the great Judaeo-Christian literature, history, and culture.

These can be very important factors in the life of an individual, and I certainly do not want to minimize them. However, I would point out that they still do not resolve our problem. We are asking whether the cross is the thin edge of a wedge by which God is going to solve all the human predicament, even for those who do not receive the forgiveness he provided there. But the above considerations apply only to men who have, in fact, accepted divine forgiveness. We happily confess that the cross goes far towards helping the individual who accepts the forgiveness it provided, and eventually it will lead to his becoming a completely good person. But does it directly help the world which rejects it? I cannot see that it does.

However, there is another view that may be taken, and that is to affirm that beneath all the diagnoses which men suggest for the human predicament lies an even more fundamental problem, the problem of the relation of man to God. Since the cross resolved that dilemma, perhaps it marked the beginning of the resolution of all the human predicament. Perhaps even now the human problems are crumbling because their foundation has been undermined. Perhaps Christ at the cross lit a fire that is destined to melt more and more of the icebergs which threaten the ship of human life.

I cannot see how this picture, marvelous as it is, can be known to be true. I certainly agree that man's relationship to God is fundamental and that Christ at his cross did resolve that problem. It is just that I cannot see how that will inevitably lead to the destruction of problems like neurosis, hunger, or purposelessness, for examples, in the entire world which includes, of course, millions of people who have never heard of divine forgiveness, let alone accepted it.

So I must reluctantly conclude that I have not been able to understand a direct connection between the cross and the total problem of the human community in the way I have seen it between the cross and man's problem of sin and guilt. But now I want to approach it from a different direction because I do believe God is concerned about all his world, and we can appreciate more the glorious victory of Christ if we bear in mind a fundamental distinction.

It is very difficult to draw the line between those aspects of the human problem for which someone is responsible and that vast web of evil for which it is not possible to assign responsibility to anyone. Some cases are clear. For example, when an intelligent adult viciously betrays a friend who trusted him, he is responsible; when a tiny child contracts leukemia, no one is responsible. Other instances are not so clear, for example, when a youth gets caught up in the criminal activities of a violent mob.

Although it is not always possible to be clear about responsibility, we have assumed throughout this book that it does exist. A line exists between responsibility and nonresponsibility whether we are able to draw it or not. I believe that God knows exactly what the accountability of each human being is. And in this book I have argued that the cross is his way of forgiving men for the sins they have committed for which they are accountable.

It does not follow from this that God is unconcerned about all the network of evil for which no responsibility may be assigned. Further, it does not follow that divine forgiveness does not have real and important implications for that evil. All that I have insisted upon is that the cross was a direct attack on the problem of sin in a way that it was not on the remainder of the human predicament.

If that is true, we are free to talk about the rest of the human problem without any illusions. First, I think God is concerned about whatever is really evil in the human situation. I feel that he is concerned about ignorance, disease, poverty, broken marriages, psychotic illness, and nuclear weapons, for example. And I feel that God is at work in the war against these problems. This is his world, the Creator's world, and he has not surrendered it to evil forces like these. Every human being is God's creation, and God has not turned any of us over to evil. As Christians, we may see God at work wherever disease is being destroyed, in the efforts of all peacemakers, in the work of all responsible educators, and in the compassionate therapy of all counselors.

Second, we who are Christians may participate in God's war against evil. We do this in part, of course, by sharing the good news of God's costly forgiveness. But we also do it as men in the world, when we feed the hungry, clothe the naked, love the unloved, comfort the bereaved, and visit the prisoner. In this aspect of the war against evil, we are, first, working with God, and, second, working with the same tools, skills, and experiences as men who are not Christians.' Our faith does not provide us with easy solutions. It does provide us with three things: a hope for the future that comes from our trust in God, a clear insight into the moral realities of the human predicament, and a high motivation to do all we can in the battle against evil. It certainly does not excuse us from the work.

The best illustration of this that comes to my mind is that of President Jimmy Carter. It is not the case that his experience of being forgiven by God leads him to evade mankind's problems. Nor does his wrestling with problems like inflation or world peace or energy mean that his experience of Christian forgiveness is irrelevant. Nor does his Christian experience provide him with a direct solution to these problems.

What is true is that as a Christian he can participate in God's battle against evil both by witnessing to God's forgiveness in Christ, as he has done, and also by attacking these problems directly, drawing upon the skills and resources at his disposal. I believe that both sides of President Carter's work are important to God.

It seems to me that if we Christians cannot admit that this is so, we will have revealed that we have a moral shortsightedness, and we will forfeit our credibility before a needy world. We should not only admit that God is active and pleased whenever goodness is overcoming evil; we should rejoice in that fact.

Two more things can be said about the role of Christians in the cosmic divine warfare on evil. One is that in the past Christians have often done well, and we can be proud of that. The other is that Christians have never done as well as they should, which should cause us shame but, more important, it should lead us to commit ourselves to do even more in the future.

Ultimately, our faith is in God. We must not elevate human resources to an absolute status. Ultimately we do not trust in this government or that economy, in this education or that therapy, for that is idolatry. Ultimately we trust in God. Just as we learned at the cross to place our own lives into God's hands, so we should learn from the cross to commit our world into his hands.

In the end, God's purposes will be done. En route to that final victory, the divine, cruciform forgiveness plays an indispensable role in God's work. The God who wins the final victory is the same God who in Christ reconciled the world unto himself.

It is in that final victory, which includes God's redemptive work in Christ, that a full theodicy will appear. We cannot finally explain evil now. It is a problem for action rather than for thought. It needs to be exterminated rather than explained. As Christians, we feel that God is at work eliminating evil and that he will succeed. For us, the great victory of the cross reassures us of that. If God can forgive us, and thereby begin to transform us, at such great cost, it is clear that he really is on the side of the right and that he will continue his work on behalf of goodness until it is complete. There are many evils I do not understand, but I am satisfied that God may be trusted because of what he did for us in Christ. The cross provides a working theodicy for me now, and I am content to await until God completes his work for a final victory. Whether we are thinking about a theodicy or about the final victory generally, it is important to remember that the God who will achieve the final victory over evil is the God who at the cross suffered to forgive sins, that his costly forgiveness is indispensable in transforming sinners into good people, and that the transforming of men is indispensable for the final transformation of the world. The final victory of good will be the victory of the God of cruciform forgiveness.

8
Conclusion

Cruciform Forgiveness and the Biblical Witness

It has been our purpose in this book to use a contemporary model to explain the meaning of Christ's death. From the beginning we have been trying to say in terms familiar to us the same thing the New Testament said in terms familiar to first-century Christians.

We have used as our model the human experience of costly forgiveness. It rings true to modern ears, and it is so acceptable to modern men that it has become a truism to say, "Genuine forgiveness is always costly."

Does this model help to explain the sufferings of Christ? It seems to me that it does. Christ, as God incarnate, experienced what he did as the consequences of man's sin to one who is good, who loves men, and who voluntarily became the victim of sin. He thereby forever qualified divine forgiveness as cruciform.

Now it is time to ask whether this theological explanation of Christ's sacrifice communicates the same meaning that the New Testament did. We shall respond to this question by looking first at the general biblical message, then at the three New Testament models we observed earlier, and finally at the life and message of Jesus as recorded in the Gospels.

1. It was H. R. Mackintosh who first suggested that the basic biblical message may be stated in terms of forgiveness, and recently John Austin Baker has argued the same point. If there were a consensus on this, it would certainly make our model seem very true to the biblical message.

Unfortunately there is no such consensus among scholars, so far as I can tell. It continues to remain characteristic of biblical scholarship that the effect if not the intention of its work is to fragment the Bible.[1] The result is that many scholars apparently believe that it is misleading to attempt to state a unifying theme for the Bible. And among those who acknowledge the legitimacy of such an attempt, forgiveness might not occur at all. It does not, for example, in *God B. C.* by Anthony Phillips, for whom the thesis of the Old Testament, and by implication of the New, is that God may be trusted in spite of innocent and inexplicable human suffering.

However, although there is no scholarly consensus that the fundamental theme of the Bible is forgiveness, all scholars probably would agree that forgiveness is one major theme in the Bible. It occurs repeatedly in both testaments, and it is central rather than incidental to Hosea, among others.

But not too much weight must be put upon this for this reason: We have elaborated the model of costly forgiveness far beyond what Hosea or other biblical writers did. We have used it to explain things for which it was not so employed in the Bible. Therefore the various biblical messages about forgiveness provide some encouragement to us in our use of the model of costly forgiveness, but they do not authorize all that we have said.

2. Now we shall compare our explanation of Christ's death with the explanations of Peter, Paul, and the author of

Hebrews.

Here, once more, we are encouraged by what we find. When Peter spoke of the new age, there can be no doubt that he meant, among other things, an age in which divine forgiveness would be available. Further, when Paul spoke of justification, we have every reason to think that he was expressing in legal terms almost the precise thing that we have called in more personal terms forgiveness. Finally, the writer of Hebrews saw Christ's sacrifice as expiation or cleansing of all sins, and thus as a provision for forgiveness.

Once more, we must not exaggerate the similarity of our modern model to the New Testament teaching. We have expressed the meaning of Christ's death differently, and we have understood it differently, than these writers. Nevertheless, we find that our explanation, though not identical to theirs because we are not identical to them, is congruous with theirs. We understand in terms of costly forgiveness just what they understood in terms of a new age, justification, and sin offering. Our model explains the cross to us as theirs explained it to them.

Because of the congruity between cruciform forgiveness and the biblical models, we find that we understand their explanation in terms of our model. We can do this without any sense of having distorted or omitted their insights into God's truth. Their unfamiliar models become meaningful to us in terms of our familiar ones. So far from our modern model having displaced the ancient ones, it has rather led us to appreciate them in a new way. The truth they have contained all along, which was doubtless clear and plausible to their original users but which is less clear and less plausible to us because we are unfamiliar with their models, becomes clear and plausible to us as we see those models in the light of our own.

3. The life and teaching of Jesus naturally have a special place in all Christian theology; so it is particularly important that we ask how cruciform forgiveness stands in relation to them.

We may begin by noting how Christ's life and teaching authorized the first models for atonement, those of Peter, Paul, and the author of Hebrews. We have no reason to believe that Christ himself either understood or communicated the meaning of his death in terms of a new age, justification, or a sin offering.[2] Nevertheless there are lines which connect his life and teaching to these models. I will mention three.

It is widely agreed that the core of Jesus' teaching was the kingdom of God. Although much of what he meant by the kingdom is unclear, it is safe to say that he was speaking of the coming of a new world in which God's sovereignty and love would extend over all men's lives. Therefore his teaching about the kingdom is the source of the idea of a new age that Peter preached at Pentecost. But to Jesus' teaching Peter added his own conviction that the new age was definitely established by Christ's resurrection and the gift of the Spirit. As we saw above, the new age was an age of forgiveness. Thus a clear line is traceable from Christ's teaching about the kingdom through Peter's eschatological preaching to the idea of forgiveness with which we are concerned.

Further, we have every reason to believe that Jesus befriended the outcasts and losers of society. This made his entire ministry look questionable to the orthodox of his day, for whom it was axiomatic that God demands holiness and therefore that his true prophets associate only with those who obey the law.

This life-style of Jesus may well have been one source of Paul's concept of justification. Jesus accepted bad people and insisted that they would enter the kingdom before the Pharisees, and God honored Jesus by raising him from the dead. Eventually it became clear to Saul the Pharisee that a man cannot be justified by deeds of the law, and he was transformed into Paul the Christian by faith in Jesus. There is a correspondence between Jesus' life and Paul's theology. A line is traceable from Jesus' acceptance of sinners through Paul's forensic message about justification to our model of forgiveness of sins.

Also, Jesus is recorded as having spoken directly of his own death on several occasions, of which the most fascinating is his institution of the Lord's Supper. At that time he spoke of his blood establishing a new covenant and the forgiveness of sins (Matt. 26:28). These two themes were picked up by the author of Hebrews who elaborated them in his own way. For example, where Jesus was rather vague about his blood being poured out for forgiveness, the author of Hebrews was specific that Jesus' blood was in fact a perfect sin offering along the lines of the offerings of the Day of Atonement. Thus a line is traceable from Jesus' words about his blood at the institution of the Lord's Supper through the model of sacrifice used by the author of Hebrews to our model of costly forgiveness.

Therefore, all three of the New Testament models we have examined were authorized by the life and teaching of Jesus. They were not themselves used by Jesus, so far as we can tell, but in the rather informal ways we have seen, his actions and ideas inspired those three New Testament models.

What I want to argue now is that, in a similarly loose way, Jesus' life and teachings, mediated through those models in the ways we have observed, authorize the model we have suggested. Our model is modern; we have never pretended otherwise. It is ours and not his. But I believe it catches for us the meaning of his sacrifice just as the three New Testament models did for first-century Christians. It does not do this by repeating his words, but neither does it ignore his words and just concentrate upon the event of the cross itself, as Hodgson said theology should do. Rather, it attempts to re-present the meaning of the cross, as Jesus and then later the three writers presented it, by doing what they all did, which was to employ a familiar model from life which made the meaning of Jesus' sacrifice clear.

What, exactly, does our theory have in common with those of Jesus and the three writers? First, we have all spoken of the cross. Second, we have all spoken in one way or another of divine forgiveness. And third, we have all tied these two ideas together, each in ways meaningful and convincing to himself.

But we cannot go much further than that, for this reason: there is no model available to us in terms of which we could speak, which would authorize us to say that we have all said the same things. That is, we cannot transcend our limitations. We cannot understand or speak without the use of models. God alone can understand the truth absolutely; our grasp of it is inevitably relative. We do grasp the truth. I believe the model of costly forgiveness is true. But it cannot transcend its relatedness to our situation. Costly forgiveness is not more than we have said, a finite model with limitations in its ability to explain Christ's sacrifice. But neither is it, in my judgment at least, less than what we have said, a model that, as far as it goes, is true about the meaning of Christ's cross and also true to the meaning of Christ's cross as that meaning was understood and communicated cen- turies ago in very different ways by Peter, Paul, the author of Hebrews, and, most of all, by our Lord himself.

That, at least, is my conclusion about the model of

cruciform forgiveness. We have taken it from modern life, not from the Bible. When, however, we take it to the Bible, we find that it provides a plausible, winsome theological explanation for Christ's sacrifice. Further, when we put it alongside the biblical explanations of the cross, we find that it is congruous with them. Finally, we find that in a similarly loose way, those biblical explanations themselves are traceable to the life and teachings of our Lord.

I find this kind of authorization of our model satisfying. Some people may not. They may insist that we must prove our model to be true with texts from the Bible, which is impossible. Or, admitting that we cannot avoid using models, they may insist that we employ only models taken directly from the Bible. For reasons I have given repeatedly throughout this book, I find this procedure unsatisfactory. I do not want to add now to my remarks about theological method. But I do want to ask some questions of critics who may take the above position.

They are questions about substance rather than method. First, is it the case, or is it not, that God invaded our world as Jesus of Nazareth? Second, did he, or did he not, experience from the inside what it is like to be a human being? If he did, then is it or is it not true that God's forgiveness, the forgiveness which Christians have repeatedly experienced for almost twenty centuries, came freely to us but at great cost to God, even at the cost of his suffering as Jesus of Nazareth the consequences of our sin, even unto death, even death on the cross? In other words, is divine forgiveness cruciform, or not? Finally, is it or is it not the case that something like that divine forgiveness, admittedly on a very limited scale and very imperfectly, occurs when, for example, a man suffers en route to forgiving a friend who has betrayed him?

I have not argued, in this book, that this model is the best, or the most true, or the most biblical, or the final model. I have said only that it illuminates Christ's sacrifice and that its light is true. That seems to me to be a modest enough claim. But the more I reflect upon the cross in light of the human experience of costly forgiveness, the more I wonder if there is not something inescapable for contemporary Christians about this model. Can a Christian in the final analysis avoid it? Can even its critics avoid it? I know that I cannot. Others will have to decide for themselves.

A Parable of Costly Forgiveness

I want to conclude this book by telling a political parable which illustrates the explanation of the work of Christ which is offered in this book. Although it oversimplifies some things and leaves some others unsettled, I believe that it touches upon the important things.

A man named Bill seizes control of a small South American country. He begins a systematic, vicious persecution of all nonwhites there. He justifies his action by saying that only whites are fully persons, and nonwhites ought to die to make the world a better place for white people. He is rational, lucid, and fanatically convinced that his way is moral and that all criticisms of it are weak sentimentalism. From time to time he feels a sense of things slipping out of control, as though he were in the grip of forces stronger than himself. At other times he knows that in fact he is in control, and he insists that his conduct is moral.

What follows below are four different endings to this story. Each one is exclusive, completely separated from the others. Each one depends on the kind of response which Bill's evil actions elicit.

First Ending. A military dictator in a distant country feels vaguely unsure about Bill's actions but refuses to condemn them. Since he is white himself and is far away, Bill is no threat to him. He argues that there are probably extenuating circumstances, and in any case everyone is entitled to his own opinions. He would be happy to cooperate with Bill if the opportunity arose.

Second Ending. A citizen of a distant country, who had never heard of Bill or of his country until the atrocities, feels vaguely disturbed about it all. In his own mind he disapproves of Bill's actions, but he does nothing to express his disapproval.

Then he hears that Bill has come to his senses, has renounced his vicious actions, and has publically apologized to those groups whom he had persecuted.

"Well done," says the citizen. "A man who changes like that ought to be encouraged. I would oppose trying to call him to account. What good would be served? Let him be, and probably he will be a better leader for having had the courage to admit the error of his ways."

Third Ending. The third response came from a professor of moral philosophy in Europe under whom Bill studied several years before. He is profoundly grieved when he hears about the atrocities. He is a sensitive, saintly man, and he is ashamed that one of his former students should behave so monstrously. He feels Bill's crimes as a personal rejection, a renunciation of all the things for which he has stood all his life.

The professor writes Bill a letter urging him to reconsider his attitude toward nonwhites. He assures Bill that he is concerned about him and that his actions are causing him continual pain.

Bill comes to his senses, renounces his vicious actions, and publicly apologizes to the people he has been persecuting. He acknowledges that his old professor's letter helped him to realize how wrong he has been.

The professor is delighted and writes Bill a letter congratulating him on his new moral commitment. He assures him that his past wickedness will be no barrier between them. He urges Bill to continue to treat all his people justly, and to do whatever he can to help the families of the victims. Finally, he offers to provide whatever guidance or other help he can to Bill.

Fourth Ending. Bill's father is deeply hurt when he learns that his son has become a vicious racist. He leaves his home in Europe and flies to his son's country where he repeatedly and publicly denounces his son's actions as monstrous, all the while calling on his son to repent.

Bill has his father tortured and executed along with others who oppose his program. His father faces his death with courage: he knew that it was more or less inevitable. His last words are, "Tell my son that I died for him." Three days later he is resurrected.

Bill realizes how horrible he has been, renounces his vicious actions, and sincerely desires the forgiveness of his father and of the others he has persecuted.

Bill's father accepts Bill heartily and assures him of his love. He reminds Bill of the high standards of conduct which will now be required of him, and he promises to stand by Bill as he attempts to measure up.

Through his continuing friendship with his father, and because of his gratitude for his father's full acceptance, Bill is transformed into a humane leader. His country becomes a better place to live for nonwhites and whites alike.

Now let me comment on the parable.

1. The response of the white dictator was no help to Bill or to anyone else. It was morally and personally a failure in

that it offered no resistance to Bill's evil and so no help to Bill.

2. The response of the citizen of a distant country was morally much more sensitive. It included opposition to Bill's crimes, though that opposition took no formal action. The citizen was delighted at Bill's repentance, though he had done nothing to help Bill to repent.

What the citizen did do was to insist that repentance be rewarded with forgiveness. He refused to insist that Bill be made to pay for crimes he had repented of. The fundamental thing in his acceptance of Bill is negative, his refusal to insist on punishment.

The citizen, unlike the dictator, is on the side of right. He has done no wrong. He has been hurt by Bill's atrocities, and he has achieved something worthwhile in refusing to become embittered. But he has not done much to help Bill.

3. The professor is the first respondent to have a sympathetic feeling for Bill's victims, a sense of personal rejection by his former student, and a sense of personal shame at Bill's ruthlessness. He is also the first to help Bill to change, which he does by writing a letter.

Bill's response is therefore more personal in this case. He has been affected by the standards and the concern of his old professor. His hope for a future good reign does not rest entirely on his own resolve to change; he also depends upon the friendship and guidance of the professor. The professor has become involved in Bill's situation in a personal way. He feels a real concern for Bill, and equally he feels a concern for what is right. His concern and involvement go a long way toward altering the situation.

The professor's work, helpful though it is, is in some ways easy for him. While it involves his feeling loss and frustration about Bill, it does not require great personal sacrifice;

his letter was written from the security of Europe.

4. Bill's father's response was unique. He voluntarily injected himself into the situation where he could most effectively change his son, which was also the situation in which he himself would be victimized by his son.

He voluntarily accepted the direct consequences of Bill's evil. Other victims had suffered these consequences involuntarily, but Bill's father voluntarily chose to come to Bill's country. The professor suffered sympathetically because of Bill's evil, but he never became a direct victim of it as Bill's father did.

In this sense, the father's act of placing himself in the situation, of working to change his son, and of accepting the direct consequences of his son's evil, was objective and unrepeatable, something he did once-for-all for Bill's sake. It was objective within the life of the father himself. Henceforth he would always be the father who had experienced this and done this for his son.

One important consequence of this objective act was that it decisively qualified the way in which he accepted his repentant son. He accepted him thus, in this way, at this cost. There are other kinds of forgiveness, like those of the citizen and the professor. But the father's forgiveness is costly, and it simply cannot be understood except in terms of its costliness. It is true that the father's sacrifice led to a distinctive kind of repentance on Bill's part and to a distinctive kind of transformation of Bill, but the important point here is that his forgiveness itself bears this particular stamp, quality, character, that it is so costly.

The father's act was good in several senses. He opposed Bill's evil. He himself acted righteously. And by his actions he insured that Bill would become a humane ruler.

His act was also a loving one. He did it entirely for his son who needed his help although he did not deserve it. And he did it at great cost to himself.

It was a healthy act. There was nothing in it of masochism because it was done purposefully, to bring about a worthwhile objective.

The father's act was effective in two senses. It elicited from Bill a response of repentance, and this in turn made possible Bill's transformation into a good person.

All of this was achieved in Bill's life without coercion. The kind of relationship which was established can never be created by coercion. And the kind of person Bill became required that he freely cooperate in his own transformation.

Bill's repentance was a response, not so much to his viciousness or to his victims, as to his father and to his act of love. Thus it stood at the beginning of a profoundly personal relationship.

Bill's transformation meant that he became the sort of ruler who treats his people justly. The resource for his becoming such a ruler was his father, not himself. It was this father with this love who gave himself in this way to establish this relationship, who made possible Bill's becoming a humane ruler. This, in turn, led to a great improvement in the country.

Was the father a substitute for Bill? He was not, certainly, in any arbitrary sense. But he did stand in Bill's place in the very important sense that he voluntarily accepted a fate which was the appropriate outcome, not of his kind of life but of Bill's, and it was that act which gave his forgiveness its distinctive quality.

What of punishment? Punishment in the context of interpersonal relationships means that a good person rejects and resists a bad person. Bill's father did this. He did it because Bill was evil, and he did it in such a way as to help change

Bill. Thus he acted toward Bill in a way that was simultane-
ously retributive and reformatory.

Until Bill accepted his father's forgiveness for his evil, he
experienced only his father's opposition to it. When he repented and accepted his father's forgiveness, part of what
that involved was that he no longer experienced his father's
opposition or rejection. Forgiveness, though it meant many
other things as well, meant the end of punishment.

There is a sense in which the Father's love had reached its
limit in his sacrifice. For one thing, there is nothing else that
can be done to change a man beyond what Bill's father had
done. If this did not do it, nothing could. Also, there is
nothing that can be added to his death that would qualify his
forgiveness any further. That he died for his son's sake is a
final description of his forgiveness. Finally, the father's act is
ultimate in that there is nothing more he can do than to give
his life, for there is nothing else a man has it in his power to
give.

Did the father have to die in this way? If he had not, his
acceptance of Bill might have been grand, like that of the
professor, but it would not have been precisely this costly
forgiveness. Further, assuming that he had once committed
himself to this work, he had to carry it through to the end.
Also, it was more or less an historical inevitability that Bill
would execute his father.

But the father was not required by any standard of righteousness or other external necessity to do what he did.
Perhaps righteousness requires that one refuse to punish a
repentant person, as in the response of the citizen, or even
that one make some effort like that of the professor to help
Bill. But no law can require a good man to make a sacrifice
this great for a bad person, even for his son.

It was not righteousness that moved the father to make this

ultimate sacrifice for his son. It was something far stronger. It was love. Love is free to choose to act for a sinner at whatever cost. In his freedom the father chose to love to the ultimate, to give up his life in costly forgiveness.

I believe that is what God did for men at the cross.

NOTES

[1] See, for example, J. L. Houlden, *Patterns of Faith* (London: SCM Press, Ltd, 1977), Chapter One.

[2] Jesus did use sacrificial imagery when he instituted the Lord's Supper, but apparently he did not develop it as the author of Hebrews did.

Bibliography

Aulen, Gustaf. *Christus Victor*. Translated by E. H. Wahlstrom. Philadelphia: Muhlenberg, 1962.

Baillie, D. M. *God Was in Christ*. New York: Scribners, 1948.

Baker, John Austin. *The Foolishness of God*. Atlanta: John Knox, 1975.

Browning, Don S. *Atonement and Psychotherapy*. Philadelphia: Westminster, 1966.

Bushnell, Horace. *Forgiveness and Law: Grounded in Principles Interpreted by Human Analogies*. London: Hodder and Stoughton, 1874.

Bushnell, Horace. *The Vicarious Sacrifice: Grounded in Principles of Universal Obligation*. London: Alexander Strahan, 1866.

Campbell, John McLeod. *The Nature of the Atonement and Its Relation to Remission of Sins and Eternal Life*. Cambridge: Macmillan, 1856.

Cave, Sydney. *The Doctrine of the Work of Christ*. Nashville: Cokesbury, 1937.

Clark, Theodore R. *Saved by His Life*. New York: Macmillan, 1959.

Culpepper, Robert H. *Interpreting the Atonement*. Grand Rapids: Eerdmans, 1966.

Denny, James. *The Christian Doctrine of Reconciliation*. London: Hodder and Stoughton, 1917.

Denny, James. *The Death of Christ*. London: Hodder and Stoughton, 1909.

Dillistone, F. W. *The Christian Understanding of Atonement*. Philadelphia: Westminster, 1968.

Dodd, C. H. *The Apostolic Preaching and Its Developments*. New York: Harper, 1936.

Forsyth, P. T. *The Cruciality of the Cross*. London: Independent Press, 1909.

Forsyth, P. T. *The Work of Christ*. London: Hodder and Stoughton: 1910.

Franks, R. S. *The Work of Christ*. London: Nelson, 1962.

Hodgson, Leonard. *The Doctrine of Atonement*. London: Nisbet, 1951.

Mackintosh, H. R. *The Christian Experience of Forgiveness*. London: Nisbet, 1927.

Moltmann, Jurgen. *The Crucified God*. London: SCM, 1947.

Morris, Leon. *The Cross in the New Testament*. Grand Rapids: Eerdmans, 1965.

Rashdall, Hastings. *The Idea of the Atonement in Christian Theology*. London: Macmillan, 1920.

van Buren, Paul. *Christ in Our Place*. Edinburgh: Oliver and Boyd, 1957.

White, Douglas. *Forgiveness and Suffering*. Cambridge: The University Press, 1913.

Wolf, William. *No Cross, No Crown*. New York: Doubleday, 1957.

Young, Frances M. *Sacrifice and the Death of Christ*. London: SPCK, 1975.

Index of Persons

Index of Subjects

191